Social Media, Ethics, and Management

Social Media, Ethics, and Management examines the transformative impact of digital platforms on organizational management, communication, and ethics. It critically explores how social media and artificial intelligence are reshaping leadership models, stakeholder engagement, and decision-making processes. Combining theoretical insights with real-world case studies from international companies, the book offers practical strategies for navigating the complexities of digital transformation responsibly and effectively. This book equips readers with actionable tools to integrate ethical considerations into digital management, build organizational resilience, and leverage social media data for informed decision-making. It addresses challenges such as reputational risks, the volatility of digital trends, and fostering a culture of continuous learning. The inclusion of case studies provides grounded perspectives, illustrating how organizations adapt to the unpredictable digital landscape. Designed for researchers, advanced students, policymakers, and practitioners, this monograph is particularly relevant for those in fields such as strategic management, digital leadership, and business ethics. This book is an invaluable resource for understanding and mastering the challenges of digital transformation in today's fast-paced environment.

Sandra Grabowska is a professor in the Department of Production Engineering at Silesian University of Technology, Poland.

Roksana Poloczek is an assistant professor in the Department of Production Engineering at the Silesian University of Technology, Poland.

Sebastian Saniuk is a professor in the Department of Economics and Management at the University of Zielona Góra, Poland.

Routledge Studies in Central and Eastern European Business and Economics

Drawing together cutting-edge research from across the region, this series presents monographs, edited volumes and ‘shortform’ books on the full range of issues, themes and topics in Business and Economics pertaining to Central and Eastern Europe (CEE).

Ukraine, the EU and Economic Integration
Opportunities and Challenges
Oleg Tankovsky

Human-Centric Values, Workforce Resilience, and Organizational Adaptability
Strategic Competencies and Industry 5.0
Sebastian Saniuk, Sandra Grabowska, and Waldemar Sługocki

The Digital Transformation of Production and Operations Management
Energy Systems, Manufacturing, and Sustainability
Radosław Miśkiewicz

Leadership, Management and Organizational Culture
The Insurance Industry
Magdalena Kraczla and Sławomir Króliczek

Social Media, Ethics, and Management
Strategy and Organizational Resilience
Sandra Grabowska, Roksana Poloczek, and Sebastian Saniuk

https://www.routledge.com/Routledge-Studies-in-Central-and-Eastern-European-Business-and-Economics/book-series/RSCEEBE

Social Media, Ethics, and Management

Strategy and Organizational Resilience

Sandra Grabowska, Roksana Poloczek, and Sebastian Saniuk

Routledge
Taylor & Francis Group
NEW YORK AND LONDON

First published 2026
by Routledge
605 Third Avenue, New York, NY 10158

and by Routledge
4 Park Square, Milton Park, Abingdon, Oxon OX14 4RN

Routledge is an imprint of the Taylor & Francis Group, an informa business

ISBN: 978-1-041-22067-1 (hbk)
ISBN: 978-1-041-22072-5 (pbk)
ISBN: 978-1-003-73050-7 (ebk)

DOI: 10.4324/9781003730507

Typeset in Times New Roman
by Apex CoVantage, LLC

Contents

Summary

Contemporary organizations are undergoing a profound transformation shaped by the growing entanglement of technological systems, regulatory pressures, and shifting societal expectations. As digital tools increasingly structure communication, decision-making, and stakeholder interaction, organizations must learn to operate within environments defined by heightened transparency, intensified scrutiny, and accelerating informational dynamics. Understanding how these forces influence managerial practice requires attention not only to abstract principles but also to the concrete contexts in which organizations function and adapt. It is in this light that the authors draw on empirical research conducted among organizations operating in European countries. This regional focus introduces a meaningful interpretive frame: the data reflect environments shaped by stringent data-protection regimes, mature governance infrastructures, and well-established norms surrounding digital responsibility. These characteristics make the European context particularly instructive, as they illuminate the tensions that arise when innovation intersects with regulatory oversight, when automation encounters ethical expectations, and when technological acceleration outpaces organizational capacity for adaptation. At the same time, the findings show how legal, cultural, and infrastructural conditions influence everyday managerial decisions and the trajectories of technological adoption.

Yet the empirical perspective offered here serves a larger purpose: it illustrates a broader transformation unfolding across contemporary organizational systems. As digital infrastructures become embedded in everyday work, communication, and decision-making, managers face a shifting landscape in which responsibilities, risks, and expectations are continuously renegotiated. The book's analyses reveal that digital transformation has created an environment where organizational boundaries are increasingly porous, where interactions between stakeholders unfold across hybrid online–offline spaces, and where the consequences of organizational decisions are amplified, accelerated, and made visible through networked technologies.

One of the recurring themes emerging from the research is the growing interdependence between technological systems and organizational cultures.

Technologies do not operate in isolation; they reshape routines, habits, power relations, and norms of cooperation. In the European context, where regulatory scrutiny is strong and public expectations for transparency are high, this interdependence becomes especially evident. Managers report that the introduction of algorithmic tools or new data-driven processes often triggers not only operational changes but also shifts in organizational identity, prompting employees to question established practices and leaders to reconsider governance structures. The research suggests that successful digital transformation is contingent on the organization's capacity to integrate technological change with cultural learning, dialogue, and ethical reflection.

Another insight drawn from the empirical material concerns the evolving nature of organizational risk. Traditional approaches to risk management—centered on anticipating discrete threats and designing linear response protocols—are increasingly insufficient in environments where risk emerges through dynamic interactions between users, technologies, and platforms. The organizations studied describe a shift toward continuous monitoring, adaptive coordination, and constant recalibration of communication strategies. This shift is partially driven by external pressures: technological infrastructures evolve rapidly, regulatory frameworks expand, and stakeholder expectations become more demanding. But it is also driven by internal recognition that resilience is not merely a reactive capacity but an ongoing organizational practice involving data literacy, psychological readiness, and ethical sensitivity.

The findings also underscore the complexity of managing organizational reputation in a digital ecosystem. European organizations operate under close public scrutiny, and reputation is shaped not only by strategic communication but also by the behavior of individual employees, algorithmic biases, platform dynamics, and societal narratives surrounding technology. Managers interviewed describe a growing sense of responsibility: not only for what their organizations say and do, but also for how their technologies behave, how data are interpreted, and how automated systems may inadvertently influence public perception. This expanded sense of accountability is characteristic of digital-era management and will become increasingly important as artificial intelligence (AI) systems take on a more prominent role in communication and decision-making.

A further implication of the research concerns the problem of competence gaps. While European organizations often possess robust regulatory and infrastructural capabilities, they frequently struggle with talent shortages and uneven digital literacy. The findings reveal that technological implementation is often slowed not by cost, but by a lack of specialized skills— particularly in areas such as AI governance, data interpretation, ethical auditing, and cross-functional collaboration. This suggests that future strategies for digital transformation must prioritize human capability development at least as much as technological investment. Organizations that cultivate interdisciplinary expertise, strong reflexive practices, and critical awareness among employees are better equipped to navigate the uncertainties associated with emerging technologies.

As the book's chapters collectively demonstrate, digital transformation cannot be understood solely as a technical project. It must be approached as a multidimensional process that simultaneously affects structures, cultures, strategies, and the normative foundations of organizational life. The conclusion that emerges from the research is that digitalization demands a rethinking of leadership at every level of the organization. Leaders must not only make decisions informed by data but also interpret these data critically, question algorithmic recommendations, and recognize the ethical and social implications embedded in technological design. They must guide their teams through increasingly complex environments in which urgency, visibility, and unpredictability intensify the pressures of managerial work.

Furthermore, the findings point to an overarching challenge: the difficulty of balancing speed and responsibility. Digital platforms create expectations of instantaneous communication and rapid adaptation, yet responsible decision-making requires time—time to reflect, assess consequences, consult stakeholders, and weigh ethical considerations. This tension is pervasive across all domains of digital management, from crisis response to content moderation to the adoption of AI tools. Organizations that learn to navigate this tension—through clear governance structures, transparent communication, and well-established ethical frameworks—are more likely to sustain both effectiveness and legitimacy in digitally mediated environments.

The book also highlights the importance of understanding digital transformation as a global phenomenon shaped by local realities. While the empirical material is rooted in Europe, the analyses situate these findings within broader international debates. Across the world, organizations face similar dilemmas related to surveillance, bias, misinformation, platform dependency, and the governance of algorithmic systems. Yet they encounter these dilemmas within diverse legal frameworks, cultural norms, and infrastructural conditions. By situating European evidence within a global conversation, the book encourages researchers and practitioners to recognize the plurality of digital transformation pathways and the need for comparative perspectives.

The findings also underscore the importance of interdisciplinary collaboration. As organizations confront challenges involving algorithmic bias, psychological safety, disinformation, data protection, and digital inclusion, no single discipline offers sufficient expertise. Scholars of management, communication, ethics, law, and computer science must work together to develop frameworks that address the multidimensional nature of digital transformation. The richness of the empirical material presented in this book precisely reflects this need: the problems encountered by organizations cannot be solved solely through technological fixes; they require holistic inquiry and multi-perspective analysis.

The final conclusion is clear: organizations must learn to operate not only with technology but also through technology—understanding its limitations, anticipating its consequences, designing its use in alignment with core values, and building structures that enable conscious, responsible participation in the digital environment. In an era marked by rising complexity, heightened informational sensitivity, and the pervasive logic of algorithmic systems, only such an approach allows organizations to function effectively, ethically, and with long-term foresight.

This requires a fundamental shift in how organizations conceptualize their relationship with technology. Rather than treating digital tools as isolated instruments introduced to increase efficiency, organizations must recognize them as decision-making, communicative, and cultural infrastructures. This shift demands a move away from a model that focuses on implementing individual technological solutions toward one in which technological reflection is embedded in the very fabric of managerial practice. Organizations must build the capacity to evaluate where automation generates genuine value—and where it risks amplifying errors, obscuring critical signals, or producing unintended societal effects. Strengthening this evaluative capability becomes a central dimension of responsible leadership.

Parallel to this, organizations must design structures that support ongoing monitoring of technological systems and enable rapid, informed responses to their outcomes. In practice, this means establishing interdisciplinary teams that integrate technological, legal, ethical, and communication expertise. Only such teams can assess whether a given solution remains aligned with organizational values, regulatory norms, and stakeholder expectations. As a result, organizations must institutionalize processes such as algorithmic impact assessments, ethical audits, incident-reporting mechanisms, and governance structures capable of detecting emerging issues, deviations, and unintended consequences at an early stage.

Another essential dimension of operating through technology is the ability to interpret data and algorithmic outputs critically. In many organizations, data are still perceived as an objective representation of reality, despite the fact that every dataset reflects processes of selection, measurement, and modeling. What a system captures as "important" depends on its design; what it overlooks may become a source of strategic misjudgment. Responsible organizations must therefore cultivate competencies that support critical data literacy: managers must understand that algorithms do not merely reflect reality—they actively shape it. Ethical responsibility requires organizations to assess how systems classify individuals, prioritize information, and filter patterns, while remaining attentive to the groups or dynamics that may remain invisible in quantitative analysis.

Ethics, in this context, is not an auxiliary consideration but the foundation of organizational legitimacy. Technology can support organizational values only when it is designed and implemented in accordance with principles such as transparency, accountability, fairness, and respect for user autonomy. This requires systematic application of "privacy by design", ongoing bias testing, assessments of social risk, and the inclusion of diverse stakeholders in consultation processes. Organizations must build cultures in which ethical questions emerge not at the end of technological development cycles but are embedded in the design, evaluation, and deployment of digital systems from the outset.

Operating through technology also implies an ability to anticipate long-term consequences of digital systems. In environments where communication decisions and operational activities are algorithmically amplified, and where errors can escalate within minutes, organizations must develop capacities for forecasting, scenario analysis, and stress-testing. These capabilities are not solely technical; they also involve social and cultural competencies—understanding user perception, reading online community dynamics, and anticipating how information spreads and transforms across networks. Future-oriented, anticipatory governance becomes a strategic necessity rather than an aspirational ideal.

At the same time, operating through technology requires building resilience—both operational and psychological. Employees must understand how systems function, what cognitive burdens they generate, and which forms of support are necessary to maintain judgment quality under conditions of informational overload. Organizations must design not only technological architectures but also architectures of work, collaboration, and decision-making that support well-being, clarity of responsibility, and deliberate reflection. This involves cultivating environments where concerns about technology can be voiced without fear and where human experience remains a key reference point for evaluating technological effectiveness.

Ultimately, technology becomes a medium through which organizations express their values and build their credibility. Decisions related to hiring, communication, moderation, personalization, service design, and stakeholder engagement all unfold today in environments where they are tracked, interpreted, and evaluated. Responsible organizations must therefore view technology not merely as a tool of operational efficiency but as an arena of ethical visibility—one that can strengthen trust as easily as it can undermine it.

Operating through technology thus requires organizations to rethink agency, responsibility, and leadership. It requires the ability to position technology not as a driver of decisions but as an element that must itself be governed, contextualized, and interpreted. Organizations capable of integrating technological fluency with ethical sensitivity and institutional foresight will be best prepared to confront the uncertainties of the digital era. They will also be best positioned to design systems that amplify—not erode—public trust, organizational coherence, and social value.

Introduction

In the context of rapid technological transformation, the foundational assumptions of management have entered a phase of profound reorientation. The digital environments in which contemporary organizations operate are increasingly complex, volatile, and shaped by accelerated information flows that continually redefine operational and strategic conditions. These environments challenge traditional managerial paradigms grounded in stability, linearity, and predictable planning. What emerges instead is a landscape in which data-driven systems, algorithmic communication channels, social platforms, and AI constitute a new infrastructural layer of organizational functioning. Far from being auxiliary tools, these technologies shape communication patterns, stakeholder relations, decision-making models, organizational culture, and the boundaries of managerial responsibility. This book was written in response to these multidimensional transformations, offering an integrated perspective on the mechanisms through which organizations interpret, absorb, and manage the consequences of digital change.

Digital transformation does not merely introduce new technologies; it recasts the relationship between knowledge, action, and coordination. The increasing reliance on automated data processing, algorithmic filtering, and predictive analytics affects how organizations perceive their environment and construct meaning. In decision-making processes, human judgment increasingly coexists with machine-generated outputs, requiring new competencies in critical evaluation, risk assessment, and the interpretation of probabilistic signals. This shift generates new tensions between efficiency and accountability, between the acceleration of processes and the need for reflection, and between the potential of automation and the importance of human oversight. The capacity to address these tensions has become a determinant of organizational resilience and legitimacy.

The book is structured around seven chapters, each examining a different dimension of digital transformation and its implications for management. Taken together, they form a cohesive argument: that effective governance in the

DOI: 10.4324/9781003730507-1

digital era requires synthesizing technological, strategic, ethical, and cultural perspectives rather than treating them as separate domains.

Chapter 1 introduces the structural characteristics of the digital environment, focusing on the features that differentiate contemporary organizational contexts from those described in pre-digital management theories. The chapter highlights several processes that fundamentally reshape managerial conditions: the acceleration of information flows, the erosion of geographical and sectoral boundaries, and the shift from linear to networked forms of interaction. It examines how platforms, data infrastructures, and real-time communication channels alter competitive dynamics, making responsiveness and interpretive capacity central capabilities. This opening chapter also discusses the increasing permeability between organizations and their external audiences, resulting in communication spaces where internal processes become visible and must be navigated with transparency and strategic awareness.

Chapter 2 analyzes the transformation of communication within organizations. Traditional models—based on hierarchy, centralization, and the clear separation of internal and external messages—are contrasted with emerging networked communication ecosystems characterized by horizontal flows, multi-actor participation, and algorithmically mediated visibility. The chapter examines the managerial challenges resulting from these changes: the difficulty of maintaining coherence across channels, the exposure of internal dynamics to external stakeholders, and the need to cultivate trust in environments where messages circulate beyond organizational control. It also investigates the role of social listening, collaborative platforms, and internal digital communities as tools for maintaining situational awareness and fostering knowledge integration. The chapter argues that communication management is no longer a peripheral function but a central mechanism through which coordination, learning, and adaptation occur.

Chapter 3 focuses on the strategic consequences of operating in environments shaped by social media dynamics. It explores how organizations can plan and act in conditions where attention cycles are short, trends emerge unpredictably, and audience expectations change rapidly. Rather than repeating content found in the chapter abstract, this section of the introduction highlights the deeper conceptual contribution of Chapter 3: the redefinition of strategic planning itself. It argues that strategy increasingly depends on the capacity to interpret weak signals, integrate them into long-term frameworks, and balance stability with adaptability. The chapter demonstrates how organizations can stabilize their identity and values while remaining perceptive to environmental change and how the analytical capabilities developed around social data can enhance not only communication but also product development, stakeholder engagement, and innovation processes.

Chapter 4 examines organizational resilience, focusing on the mechanisms through which organizations maintain continuity in environments where crises can escalate rapidly through algorithmic amplification. Rather than restating the abstract, the introduction emphasizes that the chapter offers a deep investigation of escalation mechanisms, decision-making under uncertainty, and the coordination challenges that arise when crises unfold in real time. The chapter discusses cross-functional integration, the psychological and cognitive dimensions of crisis response, and structural solutions that enable organizations to anticipate, absorb, and recover from disruption. Its contribution lies in demonstrating that resilience is not merely a reactive capacity but a systemic property built through preparation, organizational learning, and inclusive governance.

Chapter 5 addresses the ethical and social dimensions of digital management. The introduction emphasizes that the chapter not only discusses discrete ethical issues but also situates them within broader frameworks of power, responsibility, and institutional legitimacy. It analyzes how technological systems shape access, inclusion, representation, and autonomy. It considers the ethical consequences of decisions made by designers, managers, and platform operators, and how these decisions affect stakeholders in diverse socioeconomic and cultural contexts. The chapter integrates examples drawn from organizations with strong Eastern European representation, illustrating how regional regulatory and cultural environments influence the manifestation of ethical challenges and the strategies organizations adopt to address them.

Chapter 6 presents a comprehensive framework for responsible digital transformation. It argues that technological innovation must be approached as a systemic process, embedded in organizational structures, strategic priorities, and ethical commitments. The introduction highlights that the chapter analyzes how organizations align technological capabilities with strategic goals, how they integrate governance mechanisms into digital initiatives, and how they manage new forms of risk associated with data-driven operations. It also emphasizes the chapter's attention to competencies and organizational culture, demonstrating that digital maturity depends on skill development, interdisciplinary collaboration, and institutionalized accountability.

Chapter 7 extends the discussion to emerging issues related to AI and AI-generated content. The introduction notes that the chapter investigates not only the operational uses of AI but also the broader implications of integrating autonomous systems into communication, coordination, and decision-making. It explores the challenges organizations face in ensuring transparency, fairness, and accuracy in AI-assisted processes, as well as the new managerial roles associated with oversight and curation. The chapter includes case studies from diverse regulatory and cultural contexts, illustrating the global variability of AI-related risks and opportunities.

A central component of this book is the authors' empirical research conducted among organizations operating in European countries. This geographical focus must be clearly acknowledged as an important interpretive condition: the data reflect regulatory, cultural, and operational environments shaped by strong data-protection norms, extensive transparency requirements, and a well-developed discourse on digital responsibility. Working within this context makes it possible to capture, with particular clarity, the tensions that arise when organizations implement new technologies—especially those occurring at the intersection of innovation and oversight, automation and ethics, or technological acceleration and organizational adaptation. At the same time, the findings demonstrate how regulatory frameworks and infrastructural conditions shape managerial practices, highlighting the need for further research in other regions to account for global variation in technological, institutional, and cultural contexts. The resulting empirical material offers a robust foundation for the analyses developed in this book and anchors them in the lived realities of contemporary organizational processes.

The book is intended for scholars, students, and practitioners who seek to understand how management evolves in response to technological acceleration and growing ethical complexity. For scholars, it provides a conceptual framework linking strategic management, communication studies, organizational behavior, and digital ethics. For students, it offers a structured introduction to the shifting landscape of managerial work in the digital era. For practitioners, it presents tools, analytical perspectives, and empirically informed insights that can support strategic decision-making, communication design, resilience building, and responsible technology governance.

Digital transformation requires organizations not only to modernize their tools but also to rethink the fundamental assumptions of management. It demands the ability to integrate technological and strategic perspectives with ethical reflection and to recognize that decisions made in digital environments generate both operational and societal consequences. In such conditions, essential competencies include the capacity to interpret complex signals, assess the reliability of data, manage emerging risks, and cultivate an organizational culture capable of learning and responsible technological use.

The analyses presented in this book demonstrate that effective management in digitally intensive environments depends on aligning technology with values, processes with ethics, and innovation with responsibility. The theoretical perspectives, methodological approaches, and empirical findings set out in the following chapters provide a framework for developing managerial practices suited to the growing complexity of the digital landscape. They also point to directions for future research and action—directions necessary for shaping organizations that are capable of operating effectively and responsibly amid uncertainty, accelerated change, and the expanding influence of algorithmic systems.

1 Introduction to the challenges of the digital world

Characteristics of a dynamic, digital business environment

The modern economy is undergoing a fundamental transformation that is redefining the rules of doing business. The digital revolution, fueled by technological advancements, has created an environment in which traditional business models are becoming increasingly ineffective. Enterprises, regardless of size or industry, are forced to adapt to survive and thrive in this new reality. The dynamics of this environment are unprecedented, and changes are occurring at a pace that seemed impossible just a decade ago. A key element of this transformation is the widespread availability of technologies such as the Internet, mobile devices, cloud computing, and AI. These tools enable companies to expand globally, automate processes, and create personalized customer experiences. As a result, former barriers to market entry have been significantly lowered, opening the door to new, agile competitors. This leads to constant pressure to innovate and requires organizations to be constantly ready to learn and change (Saniuk et al., 2024).

At the same time, the growing role of data, which has become the most valuable asset in the digital era, is forcing a fundamental mindset shift for businesses. Traditional, intuitive decision-making based on experience and gut feeling is giving way to a data- driven approach. In practice, this means that business leaders increasingly rely on in-depth data analysis to understand the market, customer behavior, and operational efficiency. This is a key element of competitive advantage in a dynamic environment. Making decisions based on the analysis of vast datasets, known as Big Data, allows for precise trend prediction, the detection of hidden patterns, and the personalization of offerings to a previously unheard of degree. An example is the use of machine learning (ML) to analyze purchase histories to recommend products that are most likely to interest customers. These systems not only increase sales but also build a deeper, more personalized relationship with consumers. The same applies to supply chain optimization, where data from Internet of Things (IoT) sensors allow for demand forecasting and waste minimization (Saniuk et al., 2022).

DOI: 10.4324/9781003730507-2

Competitiveness in this new paradigm is no longer measured solely by financial capital or workforce but primarily by the ability to effectively acquire, process, and utilize information. Companies that can transform raw data into valuable insights gain a significant advantage over those that cannot. In this new business world, success depends on organizational flexibility, rapid response to market signals, and the ability to continuously adapt to constantly changing conditions. Companies are becoming data laboratories, where every business process is an opportunity to gather information that can be used to refine strategies. The digital revolution has changed the rules of the game, creating a new, dynamic business ecosystem dominated by innovation, flexibility, and continuous adaptation. Understanding the key characteristics of this environment is essential to effectively manage and maintain a competitive advantage. At the same time, with new opportunities arise numerous challenges that require organizations to adopt a strategic approach and be ready for change.

Today's dynamic business environment is inextricably linked to social media. These platforms are a key element of digital strategies, but they also pose a number of challenges. First, social media introduces new, dynamic communication channels. Second, they enable immediate interaction with customers, requiring companies to be constantly vigilant and responsive. Furthermore, in the world of social media, consumer opinions become public and have an immediate impact on brand reputation. Given this business environment, one of the main challenges is real-time reputation management. Negative comments or image crises can go viral within hours. Therefore, companies must have crisis plans in place, which involve the social media team. Furthermore, personalizing customer communication is crucial. Companies are leveraging social media data to create more targeted advertising campaigns. Conversely, the importance of influencer marketing is growing, requiring careful selection of brand ambassadors (Barata & Kayser, 2023).

Social media is also a tool for building customer loyalty and engagement. Companies create communities around their products, allowing for direct dialogue and gathering valuable feedback. However, growing customer expectations for speed and quality of service pose a significant challenge. Platform algorithms are constantly changing, forcing companies to constantly adapt their content strategies. In this context, monitoring trends and analyzing data are essential to maintaining a competitive advantage.

Another aspect is the need to constantly create compelling and engaging content. Boring posts don't attract attention amidst the informational clutter that permeates social media platforms. Companies must invest in high-quality visuals to stand out from the crowd. Social media is also becoming a key sales channel, enabling e-commerce directly within apps. In this way, the boundaries between marketing and sales are becoming increasingly blurred. However, the risk of data privacy breaches is also growing, requiring companies to adhere to strict regulations. In a dynamic digital environment, speed of adaptation is crucial for survival. Companies that fail to keep up with changes in social media risk losing customers. Therefore, educating and training employees on how to use social media is a priority. In this context, social media analytics is becoming an indispensable tool. It allows for measuring campaign effectiveness and optimizing strategies. Ultimately, social media has revolutionized the way companies do business, creating new opportunities but also posing unique challenges (Patwari & Vajpayee, 2024). The development of technology—especially AI and Big Data—raises a number of ethical and regulatory questions, particularly around data privacy, algorithmic bias, and accountability. In response to these challenges, governments and regulators are introducing new regulations, such as the European Union's (EU's) General Data Protection Regulation (GDPR), aimed at protecting consumers. Companies must not only comply with applicable regulations but also build customer trust through a transparent and responsible approach to data.

At the same time, technological advancements have blurred geographic boundaries, leading to globalization and decentralization. Companies can operate on a global scale with minimal barriers to entry, reaching customers worldwide. At the same time, the growing popularity of remote work and distributed teams requires organizations to implement advanced communication and collaboration tools, as well as robust cybersecurity frameworks, which are crucial for data protection and operational continuity. This global reach opens doors to new markets but also increases competition (Khosravy et al., 2023).

In this dynamic ecosystem, data has become the most valuable asset of the 21st century. This is why companies have moved away from intuitive decisions to data-driven approaches. The use of Big Data; predictive analysis; and AI and ML tools allows for a deep understanding of customer behavior, forecasting trends, and optimizing every aspect of the business, from the supply chain to personalizing marketing offers. This approach allows not only for increased efficiency but also for building deeper and more personalized relationships with consumers, leading to greater loyalty. The challenge posed by continuous digital transformation for companies is the need for constant innovation and learning. Products and services that are groundbreaking today may become obsolete tomorrow. Therefore, cultivating a culture of experimentation and adopting a "fail fast, learn faster" strategy are crucial. Companies are increasingly investing in research and development (R&D) departments, establishing partnerships with startups, and promoting creativity and independence among their employees to keep up with the pace of change.

Finally, the modern business world rarely allows a single company to meet all market needs on its own. Therefore, collaboration and the creation of ecosystems have become essential. Companies are joining forces through technological partnerships, strategic alliances, and leveraging open platforms to provide customers with integrated, comprehensive solutions. Such collaborations provide access to complementary resources and competencies that would be difficult to develop individually, allowing for greater market value creation and faster penetration into new areas. The dynamic digital environment, while rich in benefits, poses a number of significant challenges for companies and societies. One of the most significant challenges is cybersecurity. The development of digital technologies has opened the door to new threats, such as hacking attacks, data leaks, ransomware, and phishing, which pose a significant risk to business continuity and company reputation. Securing customer data, intellectual property (IP), and critical infrastructure is a priority, requiring ongoing investment in advanced technologies and employee education (Gorodetsky et al., 2019).

Another major challenge is the skills gap. The rapid pace of technological change is creating a shortage of qualified specialists in fields such as AI, data analysis, and cybersecurity. Companies face difficulties finding and retaining talent. Furthermore, the introduction of new technologies and digital processes often encounters resistance from employees who fear job loss or difficulty adapting. Effective change management therefore requires clear communication, leadership commitment, and the provision of appropriate support and training for the entire organization. Neglecting this aspect can lead to the failure of even the best-planned transformation.

The digital environment is also characterized by strong disintermediation, or the elimination of intermediaries. Barriers to entry are often lower than in traditional industries, which favors the emergence of numerous, agile startups that can quickly capture market share. As a result, companies must constantly refine their business models to maintain market position and directly reach their customers (Kour et al., 2024).

Redefining traditional management models

The digital revolution has introduced a number of challenges that undermine the effectiveness of traditional management models. One key challenge is the accelerated pace of change. Product and service lifecycles have shortened, and new technologies are emerging with unprecedented frequency. In this environment, traditional, long-term planning and rigid strategies become ineffective. Decisions must be made quickly, and organizations must demonstrate agility to adapt to changing market conditions. Companies that are unable to adapt quickly risk losing market share to more flexible competitors. The adoption of Agile methodology has become standard across many industries, enabling an iterative approach to development that allows for ongoing response to customer feedback. The key is not only speed but also the ability to anticipate upcoming technological trends. The growing popularity of digital twins allows for process simulation and testing of innovations in a virtual environment before they are implemented in real life. Long-term planning is giving way to a scenario-based strategy that takes into account diverse potential development paths (Maciaszczyk et al., 2023).

Another significant challenge is complexity and unpredictability. Global, interconnected networks, a multitude of communication channels, and growing amounts of data are making the business environment increasingly complex. Traditional, linear approaches to problem-solving are often insufficient. Systems thinking, the ability to analyze multidimensional data, and to manage uncertainty are required. In the face of "Big Data", companies must invest in advanced analytical tools and AI to extract valuable information from vast datasets. The development of predictive analytics enables the forecasting of market trends and consumer behavior with unprecedented precision, reducing the element of surprise. The application of ML in decision-making processes allows for the automation of analysis and the identification of hidden patterns that would otherwise be undetected by humans (Mourtzis, 2024). Digital risk management methods are increasingly being used, encompassing not only cybersecurity but also risks related to faulty algorithms or data errors. A modern manager must have data storytelling skills, that is, the ability to translate complex data into understandable narratives that support decision-making (Awasthi et al., 2025).

The growing importance of human capital in the digital age poses another challenge. Employee knowledge and creativity are becoming key resources. In traditional models, employees were often viewed as machine elements, performing predetermined tasks. In the new paradigm, organizations must create environments that foster innovation, autonomy, and engagement. Employees expect greater freedom, flexibility, and development opportunities, which require a shift away from bureaucratic control structures. The concept of "holacracy", though controversial, is gaining popularity as a model in which authority and responsibility are dispersed, and traditional management positions are replaced by roles. A sense of purpose and alignment with company values are becoming stronger motivators than just compensation, underscoring the importance of organizational culture. The introduction of flexible work hours and hybrid models (part office and part remote) is becoming standard, responding to employee needs and increasing their loyalty (Jack & Bayo, 2024). Internal communication platforms and project management tools like Slack and Trello create digital spaces for spontaneous knowledge exchange and relationship building, which strengthens engagement.

Finally, increased transparency and access to information pose a significant challenge to traditional, hierarchical power. Information is no longer the privilege of management. In the age of social media and internal communication platforms, knowledge is dispersed throughout the organization. This forces managers to shift from a directive management style to inspirational leadership based on trust and collaboration. A culture of openness, in which mistakes are treated as learning opportunities rather than punishment, builds trust and encourages the sharing of information. In this new paradigm, servant leadership gains importance, as managers focus on supporting and developing their subordinates rather than issuing orders. The introduction of "pay transparency" and open communication about company performance translates into a greater sense of fairness and engagement among employees. Managers who act as "knowledge curators", connecting people and resources to solve problems, become more valuable than those who merely control. Building relationships and trust is becoming a key managerial competency, which is essential for functioning effectively in an environment where information is easily accessible to everyone.

The changing digital world is redefining traditional management models, and social media is one of the main catalysts for this change. First, these media break down hierarchical communication barriers within organizations. Instead of a rigid, top-down flow of information, employees can freely exchange ideas. This promotes greater transparency and democratization of decision-making processes. Second, social media allows managers to engage employees more directly. Creating internal groups on communication platforms fosters a sense of community and belonging. Managers, instead of being mere supervisors, become moderators and facilitators of dialogue.

New management models emphasize open communication and real-time feedback. Thanks to social media, employees can quickly report problems and propose innovative solutions, accelerating adaptation processes within the company. The approach to motivation is also changing. Leaders can publicly recognize team achievements, which build a positive organizational culture. However, these changes also bring challenges. The need to manage informational noise on social media platforms is becoming a priority. Traditional management models based on control and hierarchy must give way to more flexible and adaptive structures (Fares et al., 2025).

Social media is also changing the way companies recruit and build their employer brand. Branding is moving to platforms like LinkedIn and Instagram, where potential employees can see the company culture from the inside. Furthermore, managers must learn to manage their personal image in the digital world. Their profiles become a showcase for the values they represent. Increased transparency on social media forces organizations to be more authentic and trustworthy. Traditional management models rarely paid attention to these aspects, but in the digital age, they are crucial to success. Ultimately, social media is a powerful tool for redefining management, shifting the paradigm from control to collaboration and trust.

In response to the dynamic and unpredictable challenges posed by the digital revolution, traditional, hierarchical management models are undergoing a fundamental transformation, giving way to more flexible and adaptive approaches. The first and key direction of this evolution is the shift away from rigid, pyramidal hierarchies toward the creation of flat, networked structures that facilitate faster information flow and decision-making. Traditional, functional departments, often operating in isolation, are being replaced by interdisciplinary teams whose members possess diverse competencies and are empowered to independently solve complex problems. Agile management methodologies are becoming the foundation of this change, promoting short work cycles (sprints) and continuous adaptation to changing customer requirements. In this paradigm, organizations cease to be rigid machines and become dynamic ecosystems capable of immediate response to external stimuli. The rise of technological and market complexity has made centralized planning ineffective, forcing the decentralization of decision-making and the dispersion of knowledge throughout the organization. Organizations that adopt this model often implement advanced collaboration platforms that blur the boundaries between teams and geographic locations. This shifts from micromanagement and control to building trust and shared responsibility (Vieira et al., 2024).

Another fundamental pillar of this redefinition is a shift in the approach to the relationship between management and employees. The classic model, based on strict control, supervision, and cascading instructions, is insufficient in an environment where creativity and innovation are key resources. Contemporary leadership focuses on empowering employees, giving them greater autonomy in carrying out tasks and making decisions within their competences. The role of the manager is evolving from an authoritarian director to a mentor and coach, tasked with supporting teams in achieving their potential, removing obstacles, and creating conditions conducive to creativity. This shift in mentality is crucial because it unleashes initiative and proactivity, which are often stifled by bureaucratic procedures and excessive supervision. In organizations that adopt this approach, employees feel more engaged and accountable for their work outcomes, which translate into higher productivity and innovation. Trust is becoming the currency of the new economy, and leadership based on trust and collaboration is essential for attracting and retaining the best talent. Empowering employees by giving them a voice and influence in decision-making processes builds a sense of belonging and increases their loyalty to the company.

In the digital age, where processes can be increasingly automated, human capital—understood as knowledge, skills, and creativity—is becoming the most important asset of any organization. Consequently, modern management is shifting from focusing solely on task optimization to holistic management of talent and organizational culture. Attracting, developing, and retaining highly skilled employees requires creating an environment that is not only financially attractive but also offers development opportunities, flexibility, and a sense of purpose in their work. Managers must be experts in building a culture that promotes openness, collaboration, mutual trust, and risk tolerance. It is crucial for organizations to create mechanisms for continuous improvement of employee competencies (upskilling and reskilling) so that they can adapt to the rapidly changing demands of the labor market. Flexible work models, including remote and hybrid work, have become the norm, reflecting employees' desire for a better work-life balance. A culture in which mistakes are viewed as learning opportunities rather than a reason for punishment is crucial to fostering innovation. Talent management in the new era also involves the use of data analysis to identify potential, personalize career paths, and predict staff turnover (Ruíz-Valdés et al., 2023).

Last but not least, the redefinition is shifting from decision-making based on intuition and experience to a strategy driven by data and analytics. In the era of Big-data, organizations have access to unprecedented amounts of information, which, when properly analyzed, can provide profound insights into customer behavior, market trends, and operational performance. Investments in advanced analytical tools, AI, and ML are becoming standard, enabling the automation of analytical processes and the identification of hidden patterns. Managers must develop new competencies, such as digital literacy and analytical thinking, to effectively interpret results and translate them into concrete actions. Real-time decision-making based on dynamic data analysis allows for the rapid optimization of strategies and products, providing a competitive advantage. Information is no longer a control tool but a key resource, available throughout the organization, driving innovation and enabling a better understanding of the complexities of the business environment. In this context, predictive analytics enables companies not only to respond to changes but also to anticipate them and prepare for future challenges, which is crucial in a highly uncertain environment (Tinmaz et al., 2022).

Amazon is an example of a company that has built its success on data-driven decision-making. From supply chain optimization and warehouse management to product recommendations for customers and the development of new services, every process is driven by data analysis. The company constantly conducts A/B tests to determine which changes to its website, pricing, or product descriptions yield the best results. Amazon also uses advanced predictive analytics to forecast demand and manage inventory, minimizing waste and increasing efficiency. This approach, while seemingly cool and analytical, allows for an extremely rapid response to changing consumer preferences and provides the company with a significant operational advantage.

Zappos, the online shoe retailer, has become known for its revolutionary organizational culture. In its pursuit of a flat structure, the company experimented with holacracy, a model that completely eliminated traditional management positions and departments in favor of autonomous, self-organizing "circles". Although implementing holacracy was fraught with difficulties and ultimately led to the departure of some employees, this example alone demonstrates how companies are ready for radical change to foster engagement and autonomy. Zappos is also a prime example of the company's strong focus on organizational culture and values. Customer service is a key focus, and every employee, regardless of position, receives extensive customer service training. The company believes that culture is the key to success.

Netflix, on the other hand, is an example of a company that has built its culture on the pillars of autonomy and responsibility. Instead of strictly controlling employees, the company has focused on a philosophy of "freedom and responsibility". Teams and employees have significant latitude in making decisions, and managers provide them with "context, not control". This means that instead of issuing detailed instructions, leaders clearly communicate strategic and business goals, and employees decide how best to achieve them. This culture has allowed Netflix to attract and retain top specialists who value freedom and the ability to truly influence the product. Netflix is also known for its principle of "hire the best, pay them the most, and be ready to fire them if they stop being outstanding", further emphasizing its emphasis on efficiency and continuous improvement, not just maintaining the status quo.

New forms of stakeholder relations

With the development of the digital world, stakeholder relationships are undergoing a fundamental transformation, and social media has become a key element. Traditional, one-way communication models are giving way to dialogue and interaction. Companies not only inform but also listen to the opinions of customers, partners, and employees. Thanks to social media, relationships become more transparent and two-way. First, companies can build a direct channel of communication with customers, quickly answering their questions and resolving issues in real time. This creates stronger bonds and increases loyalty. Social media is redefining customer relationships, enabling the creation of communities around the brand. Customers can share their experiences, creating authentic and valuable content. This, in turn, attracts new consumers. In this context, traditional customer relationship management (CRM) is evolving towards social relationship management (social CRM). Companies are using social media data to personalize their offerings and better understand market needs (Lampropoulos et al., 2022).

New forms of stakeholder relations also extend to employees and investors. Social media enable more open internal communication, which increases employee engagement and a sense of belonging. Companies use platforms like LinkedIn to inform investors about their successes, which builds trust and a positive image in the market. In this way, traditional, formal financial reports are complemented by more dynamic and ongoing communication. However, increasing transparency also creates challenges. Any communication error can be immediately detected and criticized, requiring companies to be more cautious and authentic. Ultimately, in the digital age, a company's success depends on its ability to build and maintain strong, authentic relationships with all stakeholders, and social media is a key tool in this process.

The digital revolution is a key driver of change. It is not only transforming business models and operational processes but also redefining the very nature of the relationship between organizations and their environments. In an era where information spreads at the speed of light and every entity has access to global communication tools, traditional, hierarchical management and communication structures are becoming obsolete. Businesses and public entities can no longer rely on the unidirectional messaging that characterized the pre-Internet era. Instead, they must learn to maintain continuous, multidirectional dialogue with the entire spectrum of their stakeholders (Ancheta et al., 2024).

Stakeholders—from employees, customers, and suppliers to shareholders, regulators, and the media—are no longer passive recipients of messages. They have become active participants, co-creating narratives, verifying information, and exerting pressure for transparency and accountability. As a result, managing relationships with them today requires significantly greater flexibility, openness, and strategic thinking. Organizations must adapt to new expectations, which encompass not only the quality of products and services but also ethical values, social, and environmental responsibility. Before the advent of the digital age, stakeholder relationships were often based on asymmetric information and controlled narratives. Organizations held most of the information about themselves and could largely dictate the terms of communication. Channels such as traditional media, annual reports, and official statements were the primary tools for shaping image and conveying messages. Stakeholders had limited opportunities to immediately respond, verify information, or engage in dialogue.

The digital revolution has fundamentally changed the landscape in which organizations operate, upending traditional approaches to stakeholder relationship management. Three key challenges stand out, forcing organizations to completely shift their operating paradigm. The accelerated flow of information is the first, posing an unprecedented logistical and strategic challenge. Thanks to the Internet, social media, and communication platforms, information spreads at lightning speed, and one-way messages have been replaced by dynamic, global dialogue. A single negative opinion, a spontaneous tweet, or a critical blog post can become a viral, global issue within hours, forcing organizations to react immediately and be constantly alert to potential reputational crises. In this new world, failure to respond or a delayed response is perceived as an admission of guilt, and silence is interpreted as a disadvantage. It is therefore necessary to create advanced social media monitoring systems and crisis management plans that will allow for the rapid identification of threats and a coordinated response before the situation gets out of control (Zhang, 2024).

A second, equally significant challenge is increased transparency and accountability. In the digital age, virtually nothing remains hidden, and the digital footprint of every organization and its activities is easily traceable and archived. Consumers can verify product reviews not only on official websites but also on independent forums and topical groups, preventing information manipulation. Employees, using platforms like Glassdoor and LinkedIn, can freely share their opinions about their employers, revealing working conditions, organizational culture, and management competencies. Activists and nongovernmental organizations use digital media to track supply chains, uncovering unethical practices such as child labor and environmental damage. As a result, organizations are subject to constant social scrutiny that goes beyond traditional audits and financial reporting. This requires significantly greater transparency, ethical behavior, and full accountability for their decisions and their social and environmental consequences.

The third aspect is the fragmentation and multiplicity of communication channels, which poses complex strategic challenges for organizations. Instead of a few traditional channels such as television or print, we now face a multitude of platforms—from LinkedIn and Twitter, through Facebook and YouTube, to TikTok, Instagram, online forums, and instant messaging apps. Each of these channels has its own specificity, unique language, different content formats, and different target audiences. Effective communication requires organizations not only to be present on these platforms but also to adapt their communication and relationship management strategies to each one. This necessitates investing in specialized analytical tools and employing experts in digital marketing and public relations (PR). These challenges mean that the traditional, passive approach to stakeholders, based on sporadic information, is no longer sufficient. It is necessary to adopt new, more active, participatory, and flexible models that treat stakeholders not as passive recipients but as active partners in the value creation process.

New forms of stakeholder relations are not an optional extra, but a strategic imperative in the face of the challenges of the digital world. Organizations that wish to survive and thrive in the new landscape must shift their focus from one-way information to two-way dialogue and value co-creation. This fundamental paradigm shift elevates relationships to a whole new level, where stakeholders are no longer passive recipients but become active partners. In the face of digital transformation, it is necessary to move away from an approach that treats stakeholder relations as a supportive function and instead embrace a perspective in which they constitute the core of business strategy. This evolution is driven by growing societal expectations for transparency and corporate responsibility. Today's consumers, investors, and employees no longer judge an organization solely on its financial performance but also on its impact on society and the environment. Therefore, building trust through open and ongoing dialogue, not just through sporadic press releases or reports, is crucial. The ability to actively listen and incorporate stakeholder perspectives into decision-making processes is becoming a determinant of organizational maturity. In this new paradigm, innovation often stems from external impulses, and the company becomes a platform that facilitates the exchange of ideas and collaboration. Instead of controlling the narrative, the organization must focus on moderating the conversation and creating spaces for authentic engagement. As a result, these relationships evolve from purely transactional to collaborative, where both parties—organization and stakeholder—reap mutual benefits from active interaction (Sarkar et al., 2025). Ultimately, the ability to manage these complex, multifaceted relationships will be a key factor in determining long-term success and reputation in the digital age.

The digital age allows organizations to engage stakeholders in processes once reserved exclusively for internal teams. In practice, this means leveraging mechanisms such as crowdsourcing and co-creation, which allow them to tap into the wisdom and creativity of distributed communities. Customers can be invited to test early versions of products, submit ideas for new features, and even co-create marketing campaigns (Lou et al., 2024). Online platforms enable the collection of opinions from thousands of people in real time, which not only provides valuable feedback but also strengthens a sense of brand belonging. This model, exemplified by the LEGO Ideas platform, not only generates innovative products but also builds a strong, engaged community around the organization.

Starbucks, a global coffee chain, is a prime example of engaging customers in innovation through a digital platform. The company launched the My Starbucks Idea platform, which allowed customers to submit ideas for new products, service improvements, and social initiatives. These ideas were then publicly available, and the community could vote on those they deemed most valuable. Starbucks actively monitored the platform, and the most popular suggestions were analyzed and implemented. This approach led to the introduction of many popular products and improvements, such as free wireless fidelity (Wi-Fi) in its coffee shops and mobile payment options. The platform not only provided the company with invaluable market data and innovative ideas but also reinforced the sense that customers were integral to the brand's success and evolution.

Amidst a deluge of information, consumers and other stakeholders value authenticity and personalization above all. Modern technologies, such as AI algorithms and Big-data analysis, enable organizations to deliver personalized messages and experiences on a scale previously unattainable. Personalization no longer applies only to advertising but also to content, offers, and customer interactions, creating the impression that the brand truly understands and responds to individual needs (Vatin et al., 2024). However, even the most advanced algorithms cannot replace authenticity. In the digital age, where corporate facades are easily exposed, organizations must show their human side. Social media activities that are open, honest, and transparent build lasting trust. Managers and employees, by sharing their experiences and values, become brand ambassadors, giving the organization a more human and credible face.

The National Aeronautics and Space Administration (NASA), the US space agency, uses crowdsourcing to engage a broad audience in its science and research missions. An example is the Zooniverse project, a platform where volunteers from around the world can help analyze massive datasets, such as galaxy images, images of the Martian surface, or gravitational wave recordings. Tasks that would take scientists years to complete are broken down into smaller pieces and distributed to millions of Internet users. This approach not only accelerates the discovery process but also democratizes science, allowing anyone—regardless of formal education—to contribute to groundbreaking research. In this way, NASA builds a community of engaged enthusiasts who become active stakeholders in the agency's missions.

The rapid flow of information online also means that reputational crises can escalate in the blink of an eye, requiring organizations to proactively and effectively manage digital media crises. This means not only passively monitoring online sentiment but also having a precise plan for a rapid and coordinated response. Being present where stakeholders are, responding to negative comments, engaging in dialogue with critics, and quickly correcting false information, is crucial. New technologies, such as social media analytics tools, allow for early detection of warning signs and taking action before the situation spirals out of control, minimizing reputational damage (Zhang & Nekmat, 2024).

Moreover, employees, among the most important stakeholders, are also entering a new era of relationships. The digital revolution, especially in the context of the pandemic, has accelerated the shift to remote and hybrid work, fundamentally changing the internal dynamics of companies. New forms of employee relationships in this context include the use of digital tools not only to maintain cultural cohesion, internal communication, and competency development but also to foster a sense of belonging and psychological safety. Project management platforms, video conferencing, and knowledge management systems (KMS) have become key tools for maintaining relationships and ensuring that employees feel an integral part of the organization, regardless of their physical location. Furthermore, virtual workspaces require managers to develop new leadership competencies, such as digital empathy and the ability to motivate teams remotely. The transition to a remote model also entails a redefinition of work-life balance, forcing organizations to implement flexible working hours and proactively support the mental health of their teams. Having a digital, transparent, and engaging internal culture is now as important as an organization's external image, as employees have become an integral part of the organization's digital ecosystem, and their opinions, shared on social media, directly impact the employer brand. Consequently, the future of stakeholder relations will be defined by an organization's ability to be authentic, transparent, flexible, and digitally savvy, which primarily applies to its relationships with its own employees.

In summary, this chapter demonstrates that social media is one of the most important factors redefining management in the digital era. Its importance extends far beyond its role as a communication tool—it has become a space for co-creating value, building brand image, and shaping relationships with customers, employees, and other stakeholders. Organizations that consciously and strategically integrate social media into their management processes gain not only greater flexibility and responsiveness but also the ability to foster a culture of openness, transparency, and authenticity.

The most important conclusion is that effective use of social media can transform traditional, one-way communication models into multiparty dialogues, in which stakeholders become co-creators of the organization's success. However, this requires new competencies from leaders: real-time management skills, sensitivity to the needs of online communities, and the ability to manage reputational risk. Social media introduces not only enormous potential for building loyalty and innovation but also the risk of crises, which can spread with unprecedented speed. Consequently, organizations operating in a digital ecosystem must treat social media as a strategic pillar of their operations. Their role in building trust, engaging employees and customers, and shaping corporate value is becoming crucial for long-term competitive advantage. The ability to engage in authentic dialogue and collaboration in the digital space will prove to be a key determinant of success in the future.

References

Ancheta, K., Le Calvez, S., & Williams, J. (2024). The digital revolution in veterinary pathology. *Journal of Comparative Pathology*, *214*, 19–31.

Awasthi, A., Krpalkova, L., & Walsh, J. (2025). Bridging the maturity gaps in industrial data science: Navigating challenges in IoT-driven manufacturing. *Technologies*, *13*(1), 22.

Barata, J., & Kayser, I. (2023). Industry 5.0–past, present, and near future. *Procedia Computer Science*, *219*, 778–788.

Fares, N., Anass, C., Shardeo, V., & Garza-Reyes, J. A. (2025). Supply chain management in the Industry 5.0 era: Strategic implications. *Benchmarking: An International Journal*, 1–29.

Gorodetsky, V., Larukchin, V., & Skobelev, P. (2019). Conceptual model of digital platform for enterprises of industry 5.0. In *International symposium on intelligent and distributed computing* (pp. 35–40). Springer International Publishing.

Jack, M. A., & Bayo, P. L. (2024). Holacracy and organizational performance: A meta-analysis of case studies across different business models. *African Journal of Management and Business Research*, *17*(1), 249–262.

Khosravy, M., Gupta, N., Pasquali, A., Dey, N., Crespo, R. G., & Witkowski, O. (2023). Human-collaborative artificial intelligence along with social values in industry 5.0: A survey of the state-of-the-art. *IEEE Transactions on Cognitive and Developmental Systems*, *16*(1), 165–176.

Kour, R., Karim, R., Dersin, P., & Venkatesh, N. (2024). Cybersecurity for industry 5.0: Trends and gaps. *Frontiers in Computer Science*, *6*, 1434436.

Lampropoulos, G., Siakas, K., Viana, J., & Reinhold, O. (2022, November). Artificial intelligence, blockchain, big data analytics, machine learning and data mining in traditional CRM and social CRM: A critical review. In *2022 IEEE/WIC/ACM international joint conference on web intelligence and intelligent agent technology (WI-IAT)* (pp. 504–510). IEEE.

Lou, S., Hu, Z., Zhang, Y., Feng, Y., Zhou, M., & Lv, C. (2024). Human-cyber-physical system for industry 5.0: A review from a human-centric perspective. *IEEE Transactions on Automation Science and Engineering*, *22*, 494–511.

Maciaszczyk, M., Makieła, Z., & Miśkiewicz, R. (2023). Industry 5.0: A new reality, new challenges. In *Innovation in the digital economics* (pp. 51–61). Routledge.

Mourtzis, D. (2024). Challenges and opportunities of the transition from Industry 4.0 to Industry 5.0. *Manufacturing from Industry 4.0 to Industry 5.0*, 97–131.

Patwari, P., & Vajpayee, A. (2024). Exploring the interplay of educational social media usage, procrastination, and subjective well-being in the context of industry 5.0 education. *Impact of Artificial Intelligence on Society*, 119–133.

Ruíz-Valdés, S., Alberto Ruíz-Tapia, J., & Carmen Gómez-Chagoya, M. (2023). Trends and challenges in the upskilling and reskilling of the workforce in the 21st century: An analysis of the strategies and results in the acquisition of skills for adaptation to technological and labor change. *Journal of Human Resources Training/Revista de Formación de Recursos Humanos*, *9*(24).

Saniuk, S., Grabowska, S., & Straka, M. (2022). Identification of social and economic expectations: Contextual reasons for the transformation process of Industry 4.0 into the Industry 5.0 concept. *Sustainability*, *14*(3), 1391.

Saniuk, S., Grabowska, S., & Thibbotuwawa, A. (2024). Challenges of industrial systems in terms of the crucial role of humans in the Industry 5.0 environment. *Production Engineering Archives*, *30*.

Sarkar, B. D., Sharma, I., & Shardeo, V. (2025). A multi-method examination of barriers to traceability in Industry 5.0-enabled digital food supply chains. *The International Journal of Logistics Management*, *36*(2), 354–380.

Tinmaz, H., Lee, Y. T., Fanea-Ivanovici, M., & Baber, H. (2022). A systematic review on digital literacy. *Smart Learning Environments*, *9*(1), 21.

Vatin, N. I., Negi, G. S., Yellanki, V. S., Mohan, C., & Singla, N. (2024). Sustainability measures: An experimental analysis of AI and big data insights in industry 5.0. In *BIO web of conferences* (Vol. 86, p. 01072). EDP Sciences.

Vieira, J., Gomes da Costa, C., & Santos, V. (2024). Talent management and generation Z: A systematic literature review through the lens of employer branding. *Administrative Sciences*, *14*(3), 49.

Zhang, X., & Nekmat, E. (2024). Retelling the past crisis: Crisis memory and its influences on organizational reputation and public responses. *Public Relations Review*, *50*(5), 102493.

Zhang, Y. (2024). A path to sustainable development of agri-industries: Analysis of agriculture 5.0 versus industry 5.0 using stakeholder theory with moderation of environmental policy. *Sustainable Development*, *32*(5), 4829–4843.

2 Social media as a force for change in management

Transformation of internal and external communication

Modern enterprises operate in a dynamically changing information landscape that has been fundamentally transformed by social media. Social media has emerged as a driving force in management, forcing a radical redefinition of existing communication models. Former, hierarchical communication systems based on one-way messaging have given way to a network model characterized by multidirectional and interactive dialogue. This paradigm shift applies to both the organization's relationships with its environment and its internal information exchange processes (Al-Quran, 2022). The new communication architecture promotes the democratization of access to information and the horizontal exchange of knowledge, which directly impacts organizational management. Social media accelerates the transition from a control structure to a culture of trust and engagement. Externally, they enable micro-targeting and precise access to niche stakeholder groups, and create conditions for co-creation of value with customers. Internally, they contribute to the disappearance of traditional information silos, supporting the concept of a learning organization and management based on collective intelligence. As a result, an organization's ability to adapt and innovate is closely linked to the efficiency of its digital communication channels and its readiness for transparent, two-way dialogue (Comito & Talia, 2023).

In the area of external communications, social media have enabled organizations to directly reach a wide range of stakeholders, including customers, business partners, and the general public. Marketing and corporate messaging has evolved from a monologue (one-to-many relationship) toward an authentic dialogue (many-to-many relationship), reflecting the shift from the traditional PR model to the two-way public engagement. Platforms such as Facebook, Instagram, LinkedIn, and the increasingly popular TikTok have become key tools for building brand image and strengthening its reputation. Companies actively utilize these channels to present their offerings and values, as well as for content marketing based on engaging storytelling. Modern external communications management focuses on message personalization, leveraging advanced

DOI: 10.4324/9781003730507-3

platform algorithms to deliver content perfectly tailored to the profile and stage of the purchasing journey of a specific user (Mueller & Rajaram, 2022).

The ability to quickly obtain customer feedback is invaluable in the process of improving products and services. Consumer opinions, expressed in real time in the form of comments, reviews, and mentions, become a valuable input into business decision-making and R&D activities. Listening and sentiment analysis have become essential management functions, enabling the measurement of brand perception and the identification of market trends at unprecedented speed. At the same time, the two-way nature of communication poses new challenges for management teams related to crisis management (Kitchens et al., 2024). Any ill-considered message, communication error, or omission can rapidly escalate, leading to a so-called viral crisis and a serious image crisis. The need to constantly monitor brand mentions (24/7) and respond quickly and precisely to consumer feedback has become a permanent, critical element of management strategy. Responsibility for consistent and effective social media communication requires dedicated competencies, the implementation of social media policies, and a coordinated strategy encompassing all digital touchpoints. Furthermore, the role of influencer marketing and building relationships with digital opinion leaders is growing, as they become key brand ambassadors or—in the event of conflict—brand critics (Joshi et al., 2025).

Internal communication has also undergone a profound transformation, moving away from traditional newsletters and formal meetings in favor of virtual collaboration platforms and proprietary social intranets. Social media are introducing innovative tools into organizations that support the horizontal and rapid flow of information and knowledge between employees, minimizing the so-called information silos. External platforms, such as dedicated groups, as well as internal social networking sites (e.g., Yammer, Slack, and Teams), are becoming interactive communication channels, contributing to building interpersonal relationships and creating a favorable communication climate. In remote and hybrid work environments, these channels are crucial for maintaining a sense of belonging, especially in the era of globalized teams, and for minimizing professional isolation, which is critical for maintaining emotional stability and productivity (Torous et al., 2021).

Management through employee engagement is gaining a new dimension, promoting a participative leadership model and agile management. Social media facilitates the integration of virtual teams, enabling social learning through discussion forums and knowledge groups, as well as the sharing of informal knowledge and best practices (best practices), which often constitute a valuable competitive advantage. Employees can not only submit ideas and improvements through internal crowdsourcing of innovation but also create their own content [user-generated content (UGC)], which fosters a culture of innovation and strengthens the sense of agency and shared responsibility for the company's success (Kar, 2021). For human resources (HR) departments, social media platforms are a tool for building engagement, motivating, and developing internal brand ambassadors (employee advocacy), whose authentic voices naturally promote the company externally. However, implementing social media in internal management requires overcoming technological and cultural barriers, such as the risk of distraction, managing information overload (infobesity), and ensuring data security and compliance with GDPR regulations. It is crucial to develop clear usage policies, promote digital hygiene, and establish boundaries between work and private life, as well as train managers in using these tools for effective change management and transparent communication of strategic decisions. Measuring the effectiveness of internal communication by analyzing activity, engagement, and participation rates is also a new challenge (Mahajan et al., 2025).

Social media play a key role as a driver of change in management, forcing organizations to adopt a more open, transparent, and flexible approach, which is the essence of Leadership 4.0 and management in the digital era. They enable the implementation of process-based organization based on real-time data and continuous interactions with the environment, which represents a shift from rigid annual plans. Analyzing information obtained from social media, within the framework of Big Data and advanced business analytics, allows managers to precisely adapt strategies to dynamically changing market expectations, enabling proactive risk management and early detection of weak signals from the competitive and social environment (Haleem et al., 2024). They directly influence the decentralization of decision-making processes, shifting responsibility closer to customer touchpoints. Effective use of these tools requires a holistic approach to communication from management, treating it as a strategic management function integrating internal and external activities, creating a coherent and resilient communication ecosystem. In practice, this means that feedback from social media listening is immediately transferred to R&D, customer service, and sales departments, shortening innovation cycles and increasing market responsiveness. This shortening of feedback loops is crucial for competitive advantage. Ultimately, social media is not just a technological tool but a new management philosophy that emphasizes authenticity, responsiveness (velocity), and continuous relationship building (relationship marketing) with all stakeholder groups (customers, employees, investors, and regulators) (Jain et al., 2024). Organizations that effectively integrate social media into their management processes develop adaptability (organizational agility), build lasting stakeholder engagement, and gain a significant competitive advantage in the digital era, shifting from image management to managing trust and relational capital. Social return on investment (SROI) is becoming a key performance indicator (KPI) (Corvo et al., 2022).

New models of leadership and reputation management

The dynamic evolution of the communication landscape, driven by the widespread adoption of social media, is forcing a transformation of traditional leadership and reputation management models within organizations. Social media has become a powerful driver of change in management, breaking down geographical and time barriers, enabling instant communication, and engaging a wide range of stakeholders in ongoing dialogue. Consequently, effective management in today's world requires the adoption of new paradigms that focus on authenticity, transparency, and adaptability (Salem, 2022).

Modern leadership in an environment dominated by social media must move away from rigid, autocratic structures in favor of transformational and authentic models. Leaders can no longer rely solely on their formal position; their authority and trust are constantly verified by employees and consumers in an open digital space (Simionescu et al., 2023). Transparency is becoming a fundamental requirement, as social media acts as a magnifying glass on all company actions and decisions. Research indicates that leaders' activity on social media directly translates into higher levels of brand trust, which is crucial in times of institutional trust crisis. Leaders who actively communicate their values, engage in dialogue, and demonstrate emotional intelligence build stronger emotional bonds, which serve as reputational capital in times of crisis (Hess et al., 2022).

In the context of reputation management, the power of social media lies in the speed of information dissemination and the democratization of voice—each single negative opinion or positive recommendation can quickly go viral and shape the perception of the brand (Atik et al., 2022). For this reason, traditional reputation management is giving way to an approach based on social intelligence (*social listening*) and data analytics. Advanced algorithms and AI tools are now essential for monitoring sentiment in real time and identifying early signals of crisis. Moreover, the growing role of AI in corporate communications—from chatbots to content generation—presents new ethical challenges for leaders. They must ensure the transparency of algorithms and maintain a human edge in decision-making and relationship-building, as it is human values, not technology itself, that ultimately shape trust and loyalty. Appropriate use of social media in corporate social responsibility (CSR) communications is becoming a powerful tool for increasing credibility and encouraging consumers to make decisions aligned with their values (Bamdad et al., 2022).

Ultimately, social media has transformed management into a process of continuous adaptation. New leadership models must be flexible, capable of combining different styles—from visionary to operational—depending on the context. Leaders and reputation managers must develop hybrid competencies: from digital awareness and analytical thinking to empathy and the ability to build engagement. In this way, social media, a catalyst for constant change, forces organizations to re-evaluate their priorities—from a focus on information control and distribution to open dialogue, transparency, and active participation in the digital, global community (Simko et al., 2021).

The authors conducted a survey from September 1 to October 30, 2025, as part of a broader research project titled "Ethical Strategies, Organizational

Resilience, and Digital Responsibility in the Social Media Environment: The Perspectives of Management and Employees of Polish Enterprises". The primary goal of this study was to deepen empirical knowledge on ethical strategies, organizational resilience, and digital responsibility, which are key in the context of the contemporary social media environment. The survey was directed at representatives of management and employees of companies directly involved in the decision-making and operational processes of the organization. The sample included 345 companies with headquarters or branches in Poland. The sample structure was characterized by diversity in terms of entity size: 246 were large enterprises, 45 were medium-sized, and 54 were small. The research tool used in the procedure was a proprietary survey consisting of 15 questions. This design enabled not only the quantification of attitudes and actions but also the acquisition of qualitative data necessary to fully understand the mechanisms of managing ethics and digital resilience in the surveyed organizations.

An analysis of respondents' responses regarding the impact of digital transformation on management and strategy in their organizations reveals a dominant tendency to consider social media as a powerful, though not fully mastered, catalyst for change.

When asked about the extent to which social media has influenced the change in leadership models within a company, 40% of respondents indicated that the impact is very significant. This group primarily comprises the largest companies in the sample, which recognize and are actively implementing a fundamental transformation toward digital leadership. Leadership in this new model requires significantly greater transparency, authenticity, and continuous, real-time communication with stakeholders from management. Nearly 45% of respondents believe the impact is significant. This includes the overwhelming majority of large companies and some medium-sized companies, which note a significant impact on communication and the need to adapt leadership but emphasize that the transformation is not yet fully complete. This indicates an ongoing, but unstructured, change process. Only 10% of respondents rated the impact as moderate. These are companies where social media is still treated primarily as a marketing tool, not as a strategic factor for leadership transformation. This means that the management of these organizations is less compelled to change their behavior and management style. The smallest group (5%) consists of entities, mainly smaller ones or those with a very traditional management model that assessed the impact as either low or nonexistent.

Another key area was the assessment of strategic planning capacity in the face of constantly changing social media trends. As much as 25% of respondents rated this capacity as very high. These are market leaders, typically large companies, with advanced monitoring systems, flexible budgets, and adaptive planning structures, allowing them to strategically incorporate digital dynamics. Another 40% rated their capacity as high. These are large companies with formal strategies that allow for a relatively rapid response to new trends and crises, although they still feel the pressure of the pace of change. Furthermore,

25% of respondents declared a moderate capacity for strategic planning. This group includes medium-sized companies and some large companies, for whom the volatility of the digital environment poses a real and difficult challenge, indicating gaps in planning processes and tools. The smallest percentage, 10%, rated this capacity as low or very low, which applies to the smallest and least digitally advanced entities.

Analysis of responses to the question about key managerial competencies shows that adaptability and data analysis are paramount in the digital era. The most frequently cited competency, cited by 70% of respondents, was the ability to adapt quickly and be willing to continuously learn. This is seen as crucial in the volatile and rapidly changing digital environment and aligns with the concept of organizational resilience. Strategic thinking in a digital context and technological understanding came second, with 55% of mentions. This competency is identified as essential for transforming new technologies and social media trends into a real competitive advantage. Finally, 45% of respondents considered data analytics and data-driven decision-making (data analysis) crucial. This is the foundation of effective management, especially in large companies that collect large amounts of data from social media and require advanced skills to transform it into strategic decisions.

The research results clearly indicate that social media has established itself as a strategic factor transforming the leadership model, far from being merely a peripheral communication tool. This is evidenced by the fact that the overwhelming majority of respondents (85%) rate this impact as either high or very high. In the context of the largest organizations, this high level of perception translates into the need to evolve toward "Leader 2.0", which must integrate transparency and authenticity with operational management. However, for 45% of respondents (who rated the impact as high but not very high), the challenge lies not only in realizing the need for change but, above all, in effectively implementing it into the organization's daily practices and culture. Conversely, the low impact assessment in small companies (5%) signals a digital leadership gap, where social media is relegated to a purely tactical role, which in the long term may negatively impact their long-term resilience.

This dynamic communication landscape directly impacts strategic planning capacity. While the sample, dominated by large enterprises, demonstrates a certain level of confidence—a total of 65% rate their adaptability as either high or very high—this suggests that these companies possess the necessary resources (human, financial, and technological) to maintain a satisfactory level of adaptability. However, the fact that 25% of companies still rate their planning as moderate indicates that the constant and dynamic volatility of digital trends (new platforms, regulations, and AI threats) poses a chronic challenge to strategic stability. This finding strongly aligns with the book's theme, underscoring a fundamental thesis: organizational resilience in the digital age must be measured not by the stability of the plan but by the speed and flexibility of its continuous reconfiguration.

Consequently, competencies, rather than planning, are becoming the key resource. The analysis reveals a clear shift in emphasis from traditional management skills to abilities related to learning and effective information processing. The dominance of adaptability (70%) and data analytics (45%) demonstrates that modern managers must assume the role of hybrid professionals, combining a deep understanding of technology with flexibility and a willingness to embrace continuous change. The inclusion of strategic thinking in a digital context (55%) alongside adaptation confirms that these competencies are fundamental to creating a digitally responsible and resilient organization, which must be capable of rapidly processing information and making ethical decisions in conditions of permanent uncertainty.

Using social media data in decision-making

Modern enterprises operate in a dynamically changing environment, where social media has evolved from a tool for interpersonal communication to a powerful source of business data and a driving force for fundamental shifts in management paradigms. Integrating the analysis of data obtained from social platforms into the decision-making process has become imperative for organizations striving to maintain competitiveness and market relevance, especially in the face of the growing role of the attention economy and digital transformation. These phenomena force businesses to constantly shift from a reactive to a proactive management paradigm. New knowledge indicates that it is crucial not only to acquire data but also to skillfully manage the interoperability of these heterogeneous datasets with traditional information systems [such as enterprise resource planning (ERP) or CRM] to achieve a holistic view of the customer and the market. This process requires advanced Big Data architectures, the adoption of a data-driven approach, and data-driven culture "at every level of the organization, which redefines managerial and strategic roles" (Iamnitchi et al., 2023).

Adopting a data-driven approach and culture is today a strategic imperative, determining an organization's ability to maintain a competitive advantage and adapt to a dynamic business environment. It is a transformational process that goes beyond the implementation of advanced analytical tools, focusing on a profound change in the way of thinking and decision-making at every level of the organization. This omnipresence of data in the life of the company fundamentally redefines managerial and strategic roles. The management staff must evolve from leaders relying mainly on intuition and experience (so-called *gut feeling*) to *insight-driven* leaders who can ask the right questions, interpret complex analyses, and make decisions based on objective facts. At the strategic level, data becomes the primary fuel for planning processes (Dearborn & Rider, 2025). Instead of extrapolating historical trends, a data-driven strategy uses advanced analytics and predictive models to identify new market opportunities, optimize product portfolios, and minimize risk. As a result, strategies become more *proactive* and *agile*, enabling the organization to respond quickly to market signals.

At the same time, at the operational level, data-driven culture requires the democratization of data (*data democracy*). This means that access to relevant, high-quality information and the core competencies for its analysis are no longer the domain of a small group of analysts but are becoming part of the daily work of ordinary employees. The role of line managers is undergoing a transformation: they are becoming data facilitators, responsible for providing teams with appropriate tools, training, and—crucially—building trust in data as a basis for performance evaluation and local optimization decisions. Employees, empowered to independently verify the effects of their work using data, gain greater autonomy and motivation, which fosters a culture of continuous improvement (García-Orosa, 2021).

Implementing this culture requires synergy in three key areas: technology (ensuring appropriate analytical platforms and systems), processes (establishing data governance mechanisms, i.e., data governance that ensures data quality and consistency), and people (developing analytical competencies and promoting an attitude that questions hypotheses based on hard data). Only comprehensive and coherent actions in these dimensions will ensure that the organization becomes fully *data-driven*, and that data—from the operational level to the management board—will become its true strategic capital (Choenni et al., 2022).

Social media are revolutionizing management, introducing a new quality to interactions with the environment and internal organizational processes. The thesis about the revolutionary impact of social media on organizational management deserves an in-depth analysis, considering its transformative potential both externally and internally. These platforms, transcending traditional communication tools, have become an integral element of contemporary management strategies, adding a new dimension to interactions and decision-making processes.

In terms of interactions with their surroundings, social media have transformed the relationship between organizations and stakeholders. Communication has shifted from one-way to two-way, dynamic, and real-time dialogue. Organizations have gained the following abilities (Deng & Shao, 2022):

1. Monitoring and Listening (Social Listening: Immediate collection of feedback (opinions, complaints, and suggestions) from customers and the market. This allows for a precise understanding of preferences, a quick response to image crises, and the adaptation of offerings to dynamically changing market expectations.
2. Shaping the Image and Building Relationships: Active and authentic participation in discussions enables the humanization of a brand, increasing its recognition and credibility, and building an engaged community (so-called brand advocates).

3. Innovation and Crowdsourcing: Using platforms to acquire ideas, opinions, and knowledge from a wide audience, which stimulates the development of products and services based on real needs.

At the same time, internal organizational processes are undergoing significant transformation. Social media, and in particular corporate communication platforms [enterprise social networks (ESNs)], are revolutionizing HR and knowledge management (Xiong & Sun, 2023):

1. Internal Communication and Organizational Culture: These enable free, horizontal communication between employees at various levels and departments. This fosters relationship-building, increases engagement, and creates a more open and supportive information climate within the company.
2. Knowledge Management: They make it easier for employees to quickly share knowledge, ideas, and experience, transforming dispersed knowledge into organizational social capital. Forums, discussion groups, and internal blogs are becoming effective tools for quickly accessing the information they seek.
3. Recruitment and Employer Branding: External platforms are used to acquire talent and strategically shape the image of a friendly and innovative employer.

In light of the above, social media is not just a marketing channel but, above all, a strategic management tool that redefines the framework for how organizations operate in the digital era, enforcing greater transparency, responsiveness, and participation, thus introducing a new quality to interactions and management processes. Effectively utilizing this potential, however, requires the development of coherent strategies, the ability to monitor and analyze data, and the management of image risk.

The role of social media transcends traditional marketing functions, becoming a key platform for building an employer's image and brand, exchanging knowledge, and developing employees, as well as for crisis management, where it ensures immediate monitoring of information flow and enables the rapid implementation of appropriate communication. This shift forces managers to adopt transparency and honesty as key communication principles and to be ready to respond immediately to dynamic market conditions. Active dialogue with audiences, initiated and maintained via social media, transcends the traditional concept of marketing communications, fundamentally transforming them from passive recipients into engaged brand co-creators (prosumers). This fundamental shift in relationship dynamics has direct and significant implications for CRM strategies, introducing a paradigm based on two-way engagement and personalization. This new quality of interaction involves creating mechanisms that enable customers not only to express their opinions but also to directly participate in processes that were previously the exclusive domain of the company.

Audiences become a source of valuable intellectual capital and innovative ideas through:

1. UGC: Customers become credible brand ambassadors by sharing their experiences, reviews, and creative product applications. This organic marketing is perceived as more authentic and effective than traditional advertising, fostering trust and loyalty to the company. A relationship management strategy must therefore focus on stimulating and honoring this activity.
2. Crowdsourcing and Co-creation: Organizations leverage open dialogue to solicit suggestions for product development, service improvements, and even new concepts. In this way, CRM strategies evolve by integrating the customer into the business development cycle, minimizing the risk of market failure and maximizing the alignment of offerings with real needs.
3. Strengthening Loyalty through Ownership: Recognizing the customer's contribution and incorporating their voice into the brand's DNA builds a strong sense of belonging and psychological "ownership" of the brand. When customers feel like important partners, this sense of partnership becomes a powerful catalyst for long-term loyalty and reduces customers' receptivity to competitive offers.

In management practice, active dialogue forces companies to adopt a proactive and responsive approach. Customer service departments are transforming into community management departments, monitoring social media channels to not only respond to problems but also identify and reward positive interactions.

A good example of a company that actively uses social media for community management, and not just for customer service in the traditional sense, is LEGO.

Social media channels are dynamic forums for interaction, consistent with a proactive and responsive approach:

1. Proactivity and Community Building (Community Management):
   a. LEGO Ideas: This is a platform where fans can submit their own ideas for building sets. If a project receives enough votes (community support), it has a chance to become an official LEGO product. The company not only responds to ideas (responsiveness) but actively encourages the community to contribute to the brand and rewards them by introducing selected projects to the market (rewarding positive interactions).
   b. Regularly running competitions, challenges, and live streams on platforms like Facebook, Instagram, and YouTube that engage fans in sharing their builds and stories.
2. Responsiveness and Active Dialogue (customer service transformation):
   a. LEGO social media teams not only respond to inquiries about missing pieces or delivery issues (traditional customer service) but also

actively monitor and engage with fan discussions, often with humor and personality.

b. Identifying and rewarding positive interactions: The brand frequently shares and promotes original and creative work from its fans (UGC), which rewards engagement and reinforces the feeling of being part of the "LEGO family", thus fostering positive branding and loyalty.

Social media channels function more as a community management department that drives innovation, increases loyalty, and harnesses customer passion to grow the brand, rather than just as a passive point of contact for complaints.

Transforming audiences into brand co-creators requires a strategic shift from communication control to communication moderation. An effective CRM strategy in the social media era is defined by authenticity, transparency, and the ability to quickly adapt to the voice and influence of its most engaged co-creators. A prime example of a company implementing the principles of authenticity, transparency, and adaptability to transform audiences into co-creators is the fast-food chain Wendy's.

While this is an example from an industry that seems very "corporate", Wendy's social media strategy, particularly on Twitter (now X), is a textbook example of active dialogue and moderation.

How Wendy's transforms audiences into co-creators:

1. Authenticity (Unique Brand Personality)

   a. Non-corporate Tone: Instead of using the bland, polite language of customer service, Wendy's has adopted a sarcastic, witty, and confident Millennial/Gen Z persona. This tone is authentic to the Twitter platform and sets it apart from its competitors.
   b. Directness: The brand isn't afraid to engage in polemics with competitors (e.g., McDonald's) or customers themselves. This creates the impression that the account is driven by a real, honest person, not a stiff PR team.

2. Transparency (Crisis and Criticism Management)

   a. Accepting Challenges: In 2017, a customer asked on Twitter how many retweets he needed to get free chicken nuggets for a year. Wendy's publicly shared a ridiculously high number (18 million). When the customer reached over 3.4 million retweets (breaking the world record), Wendy's kept its word and rewarded him, transparently demonstrating that the brand values its customer dialogue over a rigid marketing plan.
   b. Quick and Open Responses: Instead of deleting critical comments, Wendy's often incorporates them into a playful conversation, defusing the crisis with humor while showing that it's listening.

3. Ability to Adapt Quickly (Contributors' Influence on Business Activities)

   a. Listening to the Community: The most famous example is the introduction of Spicy Chicken Nuggets to the menu. The brand discontinued them in 2017, which sparked a massive, negative community backlash.
   b. Adaptation: After years of constant pleas on Twitter, in 2019, Wendy's announced it would bring back the nuggets to the menu but only if it reached 2 million likes on Twitter. The goal was achieved in just 48 hours.
   c. Result: The brand not only brought the product back but the process also became one of the most effective marketing campaigns of the year, demonstrating that the company:

      (i) Moderates communication (setting the 2 million likes challenge)
      (ii) Adapts to the voice of co-creators (restores the product)
      (iii) Rewards positive interactions (customers get what they wanted)

In this case, the customer service and marketing departments have become one, operating as a community management department that treats its most engaged fans as influential business partners.

A key element of this transformation is the use of user-generated media (UGM) data from social media, which provides valuable feedback on customer behavior and preferences, detailed product or service reviews, and the effectiveness of marketing efforts. Media monitoring using advanced analytical tools is becoming a foundation for the decision-making process, enabling the collection of valuable data essential for image assessment, early problem prevention, and actionable strategic planning. The insights derived from this analysis enable organizations to make faster and more accurate business decisions (Hua et al., 2024).

The evolution of social data utilization has entered an advanced phase, focusing on predictive analytics and deep data integration with management systems. Social media is becoming a de facto key component of the social business intelligence (SBI) environment, transforming management from reactive to proactive (Kanan et al., 2023).

The current stage of management evolution requires a shift from simple monitoring to advanced analytical models based on AI and ML. These algorithms are capable of processing vast, heterogeneous streams of social data in real time, enabling predictive modeling of consumer behavior and market dynamics. A key element is an in-depth sentiment analysis, which, thanks to natural language processing (NLP), can identify subtle emotional nuances, purchasing intentions, and user frustration levels. Such precise insight into emotions allows for micro-segmentation of audiences and mass personalization of offers. These data are directly integrated with CRM and ERP systems, enabling dynamic resource allocation and value chain optimization (Benrouba & Boudour, 2023).

The growing importance of social data as a strategic resource also presents managers with new challenges in the areas of data governance and data ethics. It is necessary to implement rigorous data quality and security policies, as well as compliance with legal regulations, including GDPR, to counteract the risk of erroneous strategic decisions resulting from falsified data (e.g., disinformation). Furthermore, transformation requires changes in organizational structure and work culture, including democratizing access to data, developing managers' analytical skills, and leveraging internal social platforms (ESNs for knowledge management and collaboration.

In summary, social media constitute a fundamental transformative force in modern management, forcing organizations to adopt an attitude characterized by increased openness, transparency, and flexibility. Their influence manifests itself primarily in the redefinition of communication, which has irreversibly shifted from a hierarchical model to a networked, two-way dialogue. Externally, this dynamic dialogue based on public engagement and continuous social listening enables immediate feedback, becoming a strategic contribution to product innovation and proactive crisis management. Internally, dedicated platforms support horizontal knowledge flow, minimize silos, and foster a participatory culture within the framework of a learning organization.

This change in the communication environment forces leadership to evolve toward authentic and transparent models, where managerial authority is constantly verified through dialogue and engagement. Reputation management has become a continuous process, based on advanced data analytics and a readiness to respond immediately. The most important strategic conclusion is the recognition of social media as a powerful source of Big Data. Implementing a data-driven culture is crucial for gaining a holistic view of the market, which enables precise decision-making, minimizes risk, and supports value co-creation with customers.

Empirical research clearly confirms that social media is a strategic catalyst for leadership change, and that adaptability and data analytics are key managerial competencies in this era. Ultimately, social media represents a new management philosophy that, through process decentralization, increased responsiveness, and the development of relational capital, is a necessary condition for achieving organizational agility and competitive advantage in the digital age. An organization's success depends on the effective integration of this digital ecosystem with its strategic functions.

References

Al-Quran, M. W. M. (2022). Traditional media versus social media: Challenges and opportunities. *Technium*, *4*(1), 145–160.

Atik, D., Cavusoglu, L., Ozdamar Ertekin, Z., & Fırat, A. F. (2022). Fashion, consumer markets, and democratization. *Journal of Consumer Behavior*, *21*(5), 1135–1148.

Bamdad, S., Finaughty, D. A., & Johns, S. E. (2022). 'Grey areas': Ethical challenges posed by social media-enabled recruitment and online data collection in cross-border, social science research. *Research Ethics*, *18*(1), 24–38.

Benrouba, F., & Boudour, R. (2023). Emotional sentiment analysis of social media content for mental health safety. *Social Network Analysis and Mining*, *13*(1), 17.

Choenni, S., Bargh, M. S., Busker, T., & Netten, N. (2022). Data governance in smart cities: Challenges and solution directions. *Journal of Smart Cities and Society*, *1*(1), 31–51.

Comito, C., & Talia, D. (2023). Pervasive Knowledge and Collective Intelligence on Web and Social Media. https://link.springer.com/book/10.1007/978-3-031-31469-8?utm_source=chatgpt.com

Corvo, L., Pastore, L., Mastrodascio, M., & Cepiku, D. (2022). The social return on investment model: A systematic literature review. *Meditari Accountancy Research*, *30*(7), 49–86.

Dearborn, J., & Rider, K. (2025). *The insight-driven leader: How high-performing companies are using analytics to unlock business value*. John Wiley & Sons.

Deng, W., & Shao, J. (2022). Empowering green development: How social media interaction influences environmental information disclosure of high-polluting firms. *International Journal of Environmental Research and Public Health*, *19*(16), 10315.

García-Orosa, B. (2021). Disinformation, social media, bots, and astroturfing: The fourth wave of digital democracy. *Profesional de la información*, *30*(6).

Haleem, A., Javaid, M., & Singh, R. P. (2024). Perspective leadership 4.0 in the era fourth revolution industrial: Comprehensive look. *Journal of Industrial Safety*, *1*(1), 100006.

Hess, A. C., Dodds, S., & Rahman, N. (2022). The development of reputational capital–How social media influencers differ from traditional celebrities. *Journal of Consumer Behavior*, *21*(5), 1236–1252.

Hua, Y., Niu, S., Cai, J., Chilton, L. B., Heuer, H., & Wohn, D. Y. (2024). Generative AI in user-generated content. In Extended abstracts of the CHI conference on human factors in computing systems (pp. 1–7).

Iamnitchi, A., Hall, L. O., Horawalavithana, S., Mubang, F., Ng, K. W., & Skvoretz, J. (2023). Modeling information diffusion in social media: Data-driven observations. *Frontiers in Big Data*, *6*, 1135191.

Jain, V., Mogaji, E., Sharma, H., & Babbili, A. S. (2024). A multi-stakeholder perspective of relationship marketing in higher education institutions. *Journal of Marketing for Higher Education*, *34*(2), 502–520.

Joshi, Y., Lim, W. M., Jagani, K., & Kumar, S. (2025). Social media influencer marketing: foundations, trends, and ways forward. *Electronic Commerce Research*, *25*(2).

Kanan, T., Mughaid, A., Al-Shalabi, R., Al-Ayyoub, M., Elbes, M., & Sadaqa, O. (2023). Business intelligence using deep learning techniques for social media contents. *Cluster Computing*, *26*(2), 1285–1296.

Kar, A. K. (2021). What affects usage satisfaction in mobile payments? Modeling user generated content to develop the "digital service usage satisfaction model". *Information Systems Frontiers*, *23*(5), 1341–1361.

Kitchens, B., Claggett, J. L., & Abbasi, A. (2024). Timely, granular, and actionable: Designing a social listening platform for Public Health 3.0. *MIS Quarterly*, *48*(3), 899–930.

Mahajan, S. K., Sharma, V., Bhattacharyya, R., & Mishra, H. S. (2025). *Interconnected world, lost connections: The amoebic world of social media*. Taylor & Francis.

Mueller, M. E., & Rajaram, D. (2022). *Social media storytelling*. Routledge.

Salem, A. (2022). The evolving landscape of development communication. *Mass Communication in the Modern Arab World*, 111.

Simionescu, M., Vasiliu, C., Şerban, C. G., Bichel, A. N., & Hudea, O. S. (2023). Towards a modern leadership: Sustainable development-oriented management. *Amfiteatru Economic*, *25*, 1024–1041.

Simko, J., Tomlein, M., Pecher, B., Moro, R., Srba, I., Stefancova, E., Hrckova, A., Kompan, M., Podrouzek, J., & Bielikova, M. (2021). Towards continuous automatic audits of social media adaptive behavior and its role in misinformation spreading. In *Adjunct proceedings of the 29th ACM conference on user modeling, adaptation and personalization* (pp. 411–414). New York, NY, USA: Association for Computing Machinery (ACM).

Torous, J., Bucci, S., Bell, I. H., Kessing, L. V., Faurholt-Jepsen, M., Whelan, P., Carvalho, A. F., Keshavan, M., Linardon, J., & Firth, J. (2021). The growing field of digital psychiatry: Current evidence and the future of apps, social media, chatbots, and virtual reality. *World Psychiatry*, *20*(3), 318–335.

Xiong, J., & Sun, D. (2023). What role does enterprise social network play? A study on enterprise social network use, knowledge acquisition and innovation performance. *Journal of Enterprise Information Management*, *36*(1), 151–171.

3 Dynamic social media trends and long-term organizational strategies

The volatility of social media as a challenge to strategic stability

Modern organizations, from government institutions to corporations and small businesses, are increasingly utilizing social media for strategic communication, PR, and marketing purposes. However, the dynamic evolution of this environment poses significant challenges to strategic stability, especially in the context of planning and implementing long-term organizational strategies. The conflict between the dynamics of social media and long-term strategy is evident in the tension between openness and control. Social media is guided by a philosophy of openness and participation, while organizational strategy strives for consistency, message control, and the achievement of clearly defined goals.

The solution to this dilemma lies in the development of organizational dynamic capabilities (DC), which are metaprocesses that allow an enterprise to integrate, build, and reconfigure internal and external competencies in response to a rapidly changing environment, such as the volatile social media ecosystem.

David Teece, one of the main creators of this concept, divides DC into three key components that are directly applicable to managing media volatility (Teece, 2023):

1. Sensing and Identifying Opportunities
    a. New Knowledge: In the context of social media, sensing requires the use of advanced Big-data analytics and AI, not just traditional social AI models that are capable of predicting not only current trends but also the potential impact of a crisis (e.g., by analyzing sentiment, influencer reach, and the speed of spread of negative content in niche communities) before the problem reaches mainstream media. This allows for anticipating changes in customer preferences (e.g., the rise of video formats like TikTok/Reels) and early detection of communication gaps.

DOI: 10.4324/9781003730507-4

2. Exploitation Chance (Seizing)

   a. New Knowledge: This capability refers to the rapid mobilization of resources to capitalize on identified opportunities. In a social media environment, organizational agility is crucial and manifests itself in:

      i. Flat Structures and Cross-Functional Teams: Instead of traditional, hierarchical communication, agile marketing and PR teams are being created that combine data scientists, content creators, and technology specialists. These teams, empowered with decision-making autonomy, can create, test, and iterate content more quickly (test-and-learn) in response to current micro-trends.
      ii. Enhancing Digital Agility: This implies leveraging social media as a strategic asset resource to increase the overall adaptability and agility of the company. Empirical research confirms that the effective use of platforms promotes both adaptability (strategy adjustment) and agility (response speed), which translates into better results in both the short and the long term.

3. Reconfiguration and Transformation

   a. New Knowledge: This is the highest level of DC, encompassing the continuous renewal of the business model and strategy. In the era of social media and digital transformation, *transformation* means not only changing procedures but also the organizational culture to be more open and learning-oriented (organizational learning). This includes:

      i. Integrating Social Media with Innovation: This implies using social media platforms to acquire knowledge, transfer information, and build social capital among employees, which ultimately strengthens the company's innovation capabilities.
      ii. Digital Maturity: An organization's digital maturity, measured by its ability to effectively adapt to new technologies, is becoming a key moderator of the impact of digital maturity on competitive advantage. Only companies with high digital maturity can fully leverage the potential of DC in a volatile digital environment, including social media, thereby increasing their resilience to disruption.

As a result, strategic stability is no longer a static state but a dynamic equilibrium achieved through continuous improvement of meta-processes. Sensing, seizing, and transforming, which allow organizations to maintain competitiveness in conditions of hypercompetition and technological instability (Alvarez et al., 2023). The volatility of social media (referred to as social media volatility or as part of the broader concept of VUCA—Volatility, Uncertainty, Complexity, Ambiguity) currently poses one of the most serious challenges to traditional strategic management. This historical model, based on stability, linear predictability, and long-term planning, proves insufficient when confronted with the digital ecosystem. This volatility manifests itself in several key, interconnected dimensions, forcing organizations to abandon rigid plans in favor of flexibility, continuous monitoring, and adaptation (Lehrer et al., 2021).

The first and most dynamic manifestation of this volatility is the extreme speed and unpredictability of trends. In traditional marketing, changing communication formats took years or decades; on social media, it happens in mere months. A prime example is the rapid shift in user preferences—and, consequently, algorithms—in favor of short-form video formats, fueled by the success of TikTok. This revolution in content consumption forced giants like Instagram (with its Reels format) and YouTube (with its Shorts) to immediately and cost-effectively modify their architectures. At the same time, the importance of authenticity is growing, with polished and overly produced content being replaced by raw, spontaneous materials. This state of affairs means that long-term strategies (e.g., 3–5 years) are inherently at high risk of becoming obsolete even before their full implementation, as communication frameworks and even visual languages can change drastically. This necessitates a shift to agile strategic planning, which emphasizes quarterly or even monthly cycles. The extreme speed of evolution in consumer preferences and content formats implies a fundamental ephemerality in communication cycles. Unlike traditional channels, where transformations took years, social media restructures norms in monthly or quarterly cycles.

Short-form vertical video, which has emerged in recent years and was initiated by TikTok before being adopted by Reels (Meta) and Shorts (YouTube), is strategically destabilizing. It has forced corporate entities (e.g., in the retail and lifestyle sectors) to immediately allocate resources from professional image production to low-fi, in-the-moment content. These examples demonstrate that long-term communication plans are at high risk of structural obsolescence even before full implementation. At the same time, there is an increasing consumer demand for authenticity at the expense of overproduced and filtered content. Trends such as the BeReal platform are forcing brands to adopt operational transparency strategies and show *behind-the-scenes* content, which radically conflicts with the methodology of traditional, tightly controlled image marketing (Baker & Baker, 2023).

Another powerful source of volatility comes from the platforms' decisions and external regulations. Key digital platforms such as Facebook (Meta), TikTok, and Instagram regularly introduce changes to their content display algorithms, often without prior detailed warning. Such changes—for example, prioritizing content from friends over branded content, or favoring video formats over photos—can drastically alter a campaign's organic reach, dramatically impacting communication effectiveness and the return on investment (ROI) of digital marketing. Furthermore, organizations must contend with new legal regulations, particularly those related to data privacy (e.g., GDPR in Europe and Apple's changes to its user tracking policy), as well as new requirements for labeling sponsored content and influencer marketing. Faced with this constant shift in the rules of the game, organizations are forced to constantly diversify their presence across channels. This is a key strategic derisking method, minimizing overdependence on a single platform, whose algorithm can suddenly undercut the effectiveness of all digital communications. The second pillar of volatility is related to external control factors from platform operators and government institutions. These decisions introduce unpredictability into the mechanics of digital campaigns. Changes introduced to content display algorithms are referred to as "algorithmic earthquakes". A classic example is the 2018 Facebook algorithm update (Meta), which prioritized content from friends, drastically reducing the organic reach of company posts. For many businesses, this meant an immediate transition to a paid media strategy, which had a direct and measurable negative impact on customer acquisition cost (CAC) metrics and overall ROI. Meanwhile, legal and technological regulations, particularly those related to privacy, significantly destabilize measurement and targeting. Apple's implementation of the App feature tracking transparency (ATT) in iPhone operating system (iOS) (starting in 2021) has limited the ability to track users, leading to lower ad targeting accuracy and difficulties in precise attribution modeling for platforms like Meta. As a result, companies are forced to reconfigure their analytics systems at considerable cost and invest in first-party data. Potential or real operational bans on platforms (e.g., discussions about banning TikTok in the United States and Europe for data security reasons) demonstrate how geopolitical regulations can eliminate entire communication channels overnight, forcing organizations to create advanced strategic continuity plans.

The final dimension of volatility is directly related to the democratization of communication. Social media has radically transformed the previous, one-way communication model, turning consumers, former employees, and other stakeholder groups into active content creators (often referred to as prosumers). While this fosters authentic idea generation, gathering valuable insights, and building communities, it also makes companies extremely vulnerable to rapid image crises. The rapid spread of disinformation (so-called fake news), hate speech, or avalanches of negative opinions (online shaming) is beyond a company's control, creating situations in which reputations built over years can be destroyed in a matter of hours. This creates a critical need for a flexible, real-time crisis management system equipped with advanced monitoring and immediate response tools. This is diametrically opposed to the traditional strategic approach, which assumed the ability to frame potential threats within rigid, predefined procedures. In the era of social media volatility, the ability to adapt and react quickly is more valuable than the most perfect, yet rigid, strategic plan (Andrade-Vargas et al., 2021).

Social media volatility forces organizations to adopt a paradigm of strategic agility. Value is generated not by a perfectly crafted, unchanging plan, but by the ability to quickly adapt and reconfigure resources in response to the constantly evolving digital, algorithmic, and social landscape (Deveikyte et al., 2022).

This imperative of agility entails a shift from annual budget planning to flexible capital allocation on a quarterly or even monthly basis. In practice, this means that marketing and communication structures must evolve toward cross-functional agile teams. Continuous monitoring of sentiment indicators and ongoing analysis of content consumption patterns are key elements, enabling early detection of both emerging threats and market gaps (Gutiérrez-Broncano et al., 2024). Effective volatility management also requires investing in advanced predictive modeling and Big-data analysis tools, thus minimizing reliance on manual interpretation. Organizations must build redundancy in communication channels, avoiding over-reliance on a single platform whose algorithm can change suddenly, which is a form of digital risk diversification. Furthermore, the ability to quickly test and scale innovative formats (so-called rapid prototyping is becoming an indicator of a company's strategic maturity in the digital age. Introducing crisis management protocols that are procedurally flexible rather than based on rigid scenarios is fundamental to maintaining image integrity. Ultimately, leadership in an environment of volatility requires cultivating an organizational culture that rewards experimentation and the acceptance of controlled error (Gruenefeld et al., 2022). It is important to remember that the risk of losing control of the narrative is an inherent cost of democratizing communication, so it is crucial to quickly engage in dialogue with critical stakeholders rather than attempting to suppress negative trends. Managing volatility is a process of continuous learning, not an achievable state of stability. Organizations that effectively implement these principles transform volatility from a source of threat into a catalyst for competitive advantage and innovation.

Building a lasting brand identity in a dynamic environment

The contemporary business landscape is characterized by unprecedented dynamics, in which digital communication channels, especially social media, play a central role in shaping brand perception. Building a lasting brand identity in such a fluid environment requires organizations to adopt a strategic approach that harmonizes dynamic social media trends with long-term organizational strategies. This is a challenge of maintaining consistency and authenticity while requiring constant adaptation. Furthermore, in this ecosystem, a brand evolves from a single-directional (firm-centric) communication model to a co-creation model, in which recipients are no longer passive consumers of content but active co-creators of meaning. This paradigm shift requires companies to move from traditional brand identity management to the concept of branding as a dynamic capability (Spry et al., 2021). This means that the ability

An adaptive approach to management in the context of digital trends

The contemporary business environment, often referred to as the post-digital era, has undergone a transformation at a scale and speed unparalleled in the history of management. This unprecedented volatility—manifested in terms of instability, uncertainty, complexity, and ambiguity [the VUCA context, or more recently, brittle, anxious, nonlinear, and incomprehensible (BANI)]—is primarily driven by the rapid evolution of digital technologies. Innovations such as ML, cloud computing, the IoT, and, most importantly, ubiquitous social media, are shortening product lifecycles, dematerializing barriers to market entry, and constantly redefining stakeholder expectations. As a result, an adaptive management approach is no longer merely an optional competitive advantage, but a critical imperative for an organization's very ability to survive and achieve profitability. Traditional, hierarchical structures and strategic planning paradigms, based on the assumption of relative predictability, are proving ineffective in this dynamically changing landscape. This forces the management staff to develop DC—that is, the ability of an organization to sense, integrate, and reconfigure internal and external resources in response to rapid market changes (Cingel et al., 2022).

This need for adaptation is most evident at the intersection of two powerful forces: dynamic social media trends and the need to maintain the integrity of long-term organizational strategies. Social media serves as a constantly operating, global market barometer, generating opinions, sentiments, and crises in real time. Organizations must respond immediately to ephemeral trends, viral narratives, and even micro-niche discussion groups to protect reputations and engage customers. This short-term, reactive dynamic naturally conflicts with the need for stability, predictability, and consistency, which are crucial for executing long-term strategies such as capital investment, technology development, and building a sustainable organizational culture. The task of adaptive management, therefore, is to create a framework that allows for agility in operations and communications while maintaining a strategic anchor and purpose, ensuring that ongoing responses reinforce, rather than undermine, the organization's ultimate vision (Taylor et al., 2023).

Digital transformation is a process of fundamentally redefining the way organizations operate, going beyond mere computerization. Technologies such as AI, especially in its autonomous forms (agentic AI), Big Data, cloud computing (Cloud), and social media platforms (social media), are creating a new operational space. This space is permanently connected, data-driven, and characterized by near-instantaneous information flow, radically shortening the response time required by the market. In this new paradigm, traditional, rigid planning structures and methods, historically based on the assumption of relative market stability and long decision-making cycles, become insufficient, even dysfunctional. Long-term plans, developed in isolation and updated annually, become obsolete before they are fully implemented, threatening strategic coherence (Grabowska & Saniuk, 2022).

Adaptive management is a methodological and cultural response to these dynamics. It requires adopting a philosophy of continuous learning, rooted in cyclical experimentation and validation of strategic assumptions. This perspective implies the need to develop operational flexibility that goes beyond mere cost efficiency, focusing on rapid response to market signals—especially those originating from social media. This means implementing agile methodologies (e.g., Agile, Scrum, and Kanban) not only as project management tools in IT areas but as a holistic organizational model encompassing marketing, sales, HR, and even finance. Implementing this agility across the entire organization enables the creation of cross-functional teams empowered to make autonomous decisions and rapidly iterate products and services. Furthermore, adaptive management requires the implementation of strategic scanning mechanisms—often supported by AI—that monitor market and social trends, transforming insights into immediate strategic guidance (so-called actionable insights), thus combining operational dynamics with the long-term direction of the organization's development (Grabowska, 2022).

Adaptive management requires a shift from a command-and-control model to supportive, contextual leadership. In an environment where data are dispersed and critical market signals (e.g., from social media) emerge at the organization's periphery, central decision-making becomes too slow. Decision-making authority, crucial for responsiveness, is decentralized. Operational teams closest to the customer and technology (e.g., social media analytics teams) are empowered to take rapid, autonomous actions within clearly defined, yet flexible, strategic boundaries. The leader's role is evolving from a strategic director to an architect of the adaptive ecosystem.

Leaders focus on:

- Designing Structures: Creating flat, network-like structures that facilitate the flow of knowledge and the rapid reconfiguration of resources (so-called network organization)
- Shaping Culture: Promoting psychological safety and an orientation toward experimentation, where mistakes are treated as a valuable source of learning (fail fast, learn faster)
- Implementing Augmenting Technologies: Integrating Agentic AI and simulation systems that not only analyze data but also proactively suggest or automate adaptive actions—for example, dynamically allocating marketing budget in response to a sudden increase in sentiment in a given social channel

In the context of the constantly dynamic and complex digital environment, the effectiveness of an adaptive management approach is inextricably linked to the implementation of advanced tools and methodologies based on AI. These instruments, going beyond traditional automation, primarily serve to strengthen the organization's strategic ability to actively respond, learn, and anticipate change.

The adaptation process, especially in the face of fluctuations in the social media sphere, is supported by solutions in three key areas:

1. Advanced Real-Time Market Analytics: The fundamental goal in this area is to convert massive sets of unstructured market data, including data from social media platforms, into strategic intelligence. The use of NLP models and advanced sentiment analytics allows for continuous monitoring and quantification of changes in sentiment and brand perception among key stakeholder groups. This mechanism enables immediate detection of anomalies—potential image crises or unexpected demand—much faster than traditional research methods. Complementarily, the use of time series models combined with social data allows for predictive trend modeling and short-term demand forecasting. This predictive capability enables adaptive adjustments to resource allocation, including marketing budgets and proactive supply chain operational management.
2. Agentic Architectures and Simulation Environments: To gain an advantage in the speed and quality of strategic decisions, it is essential to implement an architecture that supports autonomous and iterative action. The concept of Agentic AI defines systems that autonomously pursue complex, multistage strategic goals. Given a general guideline (e.g., increasing customer engagement), the agent autonomously plans, tests, measures, and adapts a sequence of actions (e.g., channel selection, content, and release schedule) based on current results, minimizing human intervention. Furthermore, multi-agent systems (MAS) and strategic simulations provide virtual testing grounds. They enable management to test decision-making scenarios (e.g., pricing responses and new product launches) by simulating the interactions of various virtual market players (agents-customers and agents-competitors). This capability dramatically reduces strategic risk by revealing second-order effects and enabling the exploration of optimal action paths before allocating capital in the real world.
3. Reinforcement Learning (RL) in Process Optimization: Ultimately, the principle of continuous adaptation is implemented through RL. This AI methodology, based on trial and error and reward maximization, is particularly effective in dynamic and uncertain operating environments. RL finds application in highly interactive areas, such as adaptive customer experience management. RL algorithms can dynamically modify user interfaces, chatbot communication paths, and product recommendation algorithms in real time. This model is not static but evolves with every user interaction, ensuring that operational processes are continuously optimized to current market dynamics and individual customer preferences.

Integrating these tools transforms an organization from a reactive entity into an enterprise powered by strategic intelligence. AI thus becomes a key strategic competency, enabling not only adaptation but also proactively shaping competitive advantage in a volatile digital market (Rostamzadeh et al., 2024). This cultural transformation, driven by decentralized decision-making, is not an end in itself but a means to maximize the value derived from advanced digital analytics. As teams gain autonomy and ownership, they simultaneously become direct consumers and interpreters of strategic intelligence.

A culture of trust and psychological safety, established through delegation, creates an ideal environment for the effective use of AI tools. Agentic AI models deliver proactive recommendations, and real-time sentiment analytics identify new market signals. However, for this data to be quickly transformed into adaptive action, it must reach teams with both the expertise and authority to immediately adjust tactics—for example, reallocate social media budgets or modify messaging in response to changing sentiment. In a traditional model, AI data would have to pass through multiple levels of hierarchy, resulting in the loss of strategic intelligence and a return to a reactive management style. Decentralization shortens this loop. It is at the intersection of a culture of trust (enabling quick decisions) and AI's strategic intelligence (delivering accurate data) that organizations undergo transformation.

As a result, decentralized decision-making strengthens AI's core strategic competency, ensuring that analytical insights don't remain mere reports but are immediately translated into dynamic, iterative actions. This allows organizations to not only adapt to changes driven by social media dynamics but also proactively anticipate them, sustainably shaping their competitive advantage. Adaptive culture and strategic AI intelligence are thus becoming mutually reinforcing pillars of modern management (Mueller-Bloch et al., 2024).

Adaptive management, striving for maximum market responsiveness, cannot disregard a framework of long-term responsibility and corporate governance. Integrating ethical and ESG risk considerations is becoming a strategic imperative, providing a critical anchor for digital adaptation. Dynamic operational agility must be balanced with ethical principles and corporate governance rules to avoid generating short-term benefits at the expense of lasting reputation and stakeholder trust. Without this strategic framework, rapid decisions made by decentralized teams or autonomous AI systems can lead to unintended consequences and violations of social values, ultimately undermining the organization's long-term legitimacy and business stability. Thus, digital adaptability becomes a measure not only of efficiency but also of a company's ethical integrity and responsibility.

The rapid adaptation and autonomous operation of AI tools generate new, complex risks that must be proactively managed as part of a long-term strategy. Autonomous adaptive systems, particularly agentic AI making real-time decisions in the social media environment (e.g., regarding audience profiling, dynamic targeting, or content moderation), carry the risk of unconsciously replicating or escalating biases inherent in training datasets. Such uncontrolled algorithmic errors can lead to social exclusion, discrimination, or the erosion of customer trust, which is destructive to brand equity in the long term. Therefore, an adaptive organization must incorporate robust AI governance mechanisms. This requires implementing algorithmic audit procedures and ensuring transparency and explainability of critical AI decisions. Compliance with increasing regulations, such as the European AI Act, is no longer just a legal requirement but is becoming a strategic element in building credibility and minimizing regulatory risk (Doya et al., 2022).

Social media, acting as a global social control mechanism, provides a platform where an organization's ESG activities are immediately verified and assessed. Adaptive management must be able to monitor and quickly respond not only to traditional image crises but also to narratives regarding greenwashing, labor rights violations, and unethical practices in the supply chain. Adaptability in this context means the ability to verify operational data quickly and to communicate social and environmental responsibility activities authentically and transparently. Using AI to monitor the supply chain for compliance with ESG criteria and integrating this data into public communication is critical. Long-term strategic coherence requires that dynamic adaptation to digital trends be firmly anchored in principles of responsibility, ensuring not only regulatory compliance but, above all, the organization's enduring social and financial legitimacy. Adaptability therefore becomes a full-fledged capability that encompasses both market speed and ethical integrity.

References

Aimé, I. (2023). The dynamic construction of brand storytelling. *Journal of Strategic Marketing*, *31*(7), 1243–1262.

Alvarez, F., Lippi, F., & Souganidis, P. (2023). Price setting with strategic complementarities as a mean field game. *Econometrica*, *91*(6), 2005–2039.

Andrade-Vargas, L., Iriarte-Solano, M., Rivera-Rogel, D., & Yunga-Godoy, D. (2021). Young people and social networks: Between the democratization of knowledge and digital inequality. *Comunicar: Media Education Research Journal*, *29*(69), 79–89.

Baker, C., & Baker, D. (2023). *An influencer's world: A behind-the-scenes look at social media influencers and creators*. University of Iowa Press.

Brooks, G., Drenten, J., & Piskorski, M. J. (2021). Influencer celebrification: How social media influencers acquire celebrity capital. *Journal of Advertising*, *50*(5), 528–547.

Cingel, D. P., Carter, M. C., & Krause, H. V. (2022). Social media and self-esteem. *Current Opinion in Psychology*, *45*, 101304.

Deveikyte, J., Geman, H., Piccari, C., & Provetti, A. (2022). A sentiment analysis approach to the prediction of market volatility. *Frontiers in Artificial Intelligence*, *5*, 836809.

Doya, K., Ema, A., Kitano, H., Sakagami, M., & Russell, S. (2022). Social impact and governance of AI and neurotechnologies. *Neural Networks*, *152*, 542–554.

Grabowska, S. (2022). Key components of the business model in an Industry 5.0 environment. Scientific Papers. *Organization and Management/Silesian University of Technology*, *158*, 191–199.

Grabowska, S., & Saniuk, S. (2022). Assessment of the competitiveness and effectiveness of an open business model in the industry 4.0 environment. *Journal of Open Innovation: Technology, Market, and Complexity*, *8*(1), 57.

Gruenefeld, U., Auda, J., Mathis, F., Schneegass, S., Khamis, M., Gugenheimer, J., & Mayer, S. (2022). VRception: Rapid prototyping of cross-reality systems in virtual reality. In *Proceedings of the 2022 CHI conference on human factors in computing systems* (pp. 1–15). Association for Computing Machinery (ACM).

Gutiérrez-Broncano, S., Rubio-Andrés, M., Jiménez-Estévez, P., & Opute, J. (2024). Cross-functional teams. In *Lean manufacturing in Latin America: Concepts, methodologies and applications* (pp. 515–538). Springer Nature Switzerland.

Hasanah, I., Hefniy, H., & Zaini, A. W. (2023). Strengthening brand identity: Embracing local wisdom through character education management. *Indonesian Journal of Education and Social Studies*, *2*(2), 83–94.

Kulesza, W., Dolinski, D., Kosim, M., Grzyb, T., Muniak, P., & Jemielniak, D. (2022). The chameleon effect, the temporal aspects of mimicry and their impact on service measurement. *European Review of Applied Psychology*, *72*(4), 100767.

Lehrer, S., Xie, T., & Zhang, X. (2021). Social media sentiment, uncertainty model, and volatility forecasting. *Economic Modeling*, *102*, 105556.

Mueller-Bloch, C., Andersen, J. V., Spasovski, J., & Hahn, J. (2024). Understanding decentralization of decision-making power in proof-of-stake blockchains: An agent-based simulation approach. *European Journal of Information Systems*, *33*(3), 267–286.

Parris, D. L., & Guzmán, F. (2023). Evolving brand boundaries and expectations: Looking back on brand equity, brand loyalty, and brand image research to move forward. *Journal of Product & Brand Management*, *32*(2), 191–234.

Rostamzadeh, R., Nikic, M., Abdsharafat, M., Baghirov, F., & Khouri, S. (2024). Evaluating the impact of future studies on organizational strategic intelligence. *Transformations in Business & Economics*, *23*(3).

Solomon, M. R. (2022). Digital identity: The postmodern consumer Chameleon. In *The Routledge handbook of digital consumption* (pp. 86–97). Routledge.

Spry, A., Figueiredo, B., Gurrieri, L., Kemper, J. A., & Vredenburg, J. (2021). Transformative branding: A dynamic capability to challenge the dominant social paradigm. *Journal of Macromarketing*, *41*(4), 531–546.

Taylor, S. J., Muchnik, L., Kumar, M., & Aral, S. (2023). Identity effects in social media. *Nature Human Behavior*, *7*(1), 27–37.

Teece, D. J. (2023). The evolution of the dynamic capabilities framework. *Artificiality and Sustainability in Entrepreneurship*, *113*, 238.

Whitler, K. A., Rego, L. L., & Morgan, N. A. (2025). Chief marketing officer role design. *Journal of the Academy of Marketing Science*, 1–22.

4 The framework of organizational resilience in the context of social media

Real-time crisis management

The contemporary operating environment is characterized by increased unpredictability and interconnectedness, making real-time crisis management a key element of organizational resilience frameworks. In the era of social media dominance, the dynamics of crisis emergence and escalation have fundamentally changed, requiring organizations to adapt their strategies and tools. Platforms such as X (formerly Twitter), Facebook, and Instagram have transformed from communication tools into powerful, global early warning systems and crisis accelerators. Information, whether true or false, spreads at unprecedented speed, creating the phenomenon of "whirling crisis". In this context, real-time management is no longer an option but an imperative. It encompasses not only rapid response but, above all, continuous monitoring, sentiment analysis, and immediate fact-checking. The ability to absorb, adapt, and recover from shocks is the definition of organizational resilience (Martín-Rojas et al., 2023).

Continuing the analysis of the research conducted by the authors (described in Chapter 2), we present a detailed description of the results for questions regarding organizational resilience and crisis management in the digital environment. When asked if your company has formal, documented procedures for managing reputational crises in real time using social media, the overwhelming majority of surveyed companies declared that they do exist. In this regard, 60% of respondents responded "yes", which directly reflects the sample structure, which is dominated by large enterprises, for which high reputational risk necessitates formalized actions. Having documented procedures indicates a high level of preparedness and awareness of the need for a rapid response, providing the foundation for organizational resilience in the digital age. On the other hand, 40% of respondents responded "no" or "in development". This group, primarily comprised of smaller companies and those less digitally advanced, relies on informal, reactive measures. The lack of formal protocols in this group means a higher risk of crisis escalation and lower operational effectiveness in situations where social media response time is critical.

DOI: 10.4324/9781003730507-5

Crisis formalization is the norm in large enterprises, but not universally accepted. The persistently high percentage of companies without these procedures (40%) highlights gaps in operational readiness for real-time crisis management, directly compromising their resilience in times of sudden volatility.

In the context of the social media crisis, this resilience manifests itself through three main pillars that translate into effective management in a dynamic environment (Chen & Liu, 2025):

1. Anticipation and Preparation (Absorption): This includes ongoing team training, creating integrated crisis communication plans that take into account the specifics of each platform, and crisis simulations (so-called *dark posts* and *dark sites* prepared in advance). Social media monitoring systems must be integrated with the crisis operations center, enabling immediate detection of anomalies in discussion patterns.
2. Rapid Decision-Making and Adaptation: The social media crisis requires decentralized decision-making within established protocols. Teams must be empowered to formulate and publish initial messages without unnecessary delay, while maintaining consistency with the overarching strategy. Communicating clearly and empathetically is crucial, often using platform-native language and formats (e.g., short videos and graphics).
3. Learning and Recovery: Once the most acute phase has subsided, it's crucial to conduct a thorough post-crisis analysis to verify the effectiveness of implemented protocols in real time. Organizations must learn how social media audiences respond to crises affecting their industry and how to optimize algorithms and communication channels to quickly regain trust and reputation.

Implementing these resilience pillars requires adopting a specific, structured framework that provides a practical guide for managing social media crises in real time. This framework, based on a continuous cycle of listening, analysis, action, and dialogue, is essential for managing the dynamics of a "swirling crisis":

- 24/7 Monitoring (Listening): Using advanced tools to track mentions, trends, and identify key influencers. Identifying the tipping point where a discussion transitions from an incident to a full-blown crisis.
- Classification and Escalation (Analysis): Quickly assign a priority level and potential reputation impact, which determines the need to involve appropriate management levels (e.g., board)
- Activate Communication Protocol (Action): Activate pre-defined messages ("prepared statement") ideally within 15–30 minutes of escalation, emphasizing that the organization is aware of the situation and is actively managing it

- Engagement (Dialogue): Interact with users, answer questions, and correct misinformation. Instead of avoiding discussion, it should be monitored and moderated transparently and professionally.

In summary, organizational resilience in the context of real-time crisis management on social media relies on a continuous cycle of anticipation, rapid response, transparency, and learning. This is a constant effort to minimize the period during which the organization is vulnerable to reputational and operational damage.

A key challenge in real-time crisis management is identifying the so-called bifurcation point—the moment at which an incident (a local complaint or a single error) irreversibly escalates into a widespread crisis. In the context of social media, this point is often reached not through scale but through the authority of a source (e.g., an influential influencer or a journalist) or through the emotional resonance of a message. The framework necessary for a rapid response is the ability to sense-make—that is, to give meaning and interpretation to incomplete, often contradictory data that emerges in avalanche. In traditional crisis management, this was the task of analysts.

Today, this process must be supported by advanced linguistic analytics and AI, which (Rammane et al., 2021) point out, enables, among other things:

- Weak Signals: Detects anomalies in mention volume or changes in sentiment around specific phrases before they reach critical mass
- Classifies Tone and Emotion: Distinguishes constructive criticism from intentional attacks (trolling and botting), which allows for resource allocation in response to real threats

Organizational resilience must account for the dynamic nature of social media platforms' algorithms. These algorithms are designed to maximize engagement, which often means that emotive content—including crisis narratives, controversies, disinformation, and fake news- is promoted and reaches a wider audience faster than official messages. This is the phenomenon of algorithmic crisis amplification.

In this context, real-time management must integrate elements of combating the infodemic (Aïmeur et al., 2023):

- Fact-Checking: Establishing an immediate verification protocol. If deepfakes or doctored documents emerge, organizations must have the technical means to quickly prove their falsity and work with platforms to limit their reach.
- Source Neutralization: Develop a strategy to engage credible third parties (e.g., independent experts or industry media) to authoritatively correct false narratives, rather than relying solely on your own potentially biased statements

Contemporary crisis management in the context of organizational resilience requires a fundamental shift in strategy from a reactive model to one of continuous anticipation and adaptation. The era of social media dominance has imposed a unique, dual-track nature of crises—cyber-physical—where content generated in the digital space immediately produces tangible consequences in the operational, legal, and financial spheres, forcing organizations to achieve real-time management mastery. A key challenge in this dynamic is sensemaking, or the ability to quickly interpret the incomplete, chaotic, and often deliberately contradictory data that rapidly appears online. Effective resilience is demonstrated through the integration of 24/7 monitoring systems with advanced linguistic analytics and AI, whose task is not only to track the volume of mentions but, above all, to identify weak signals and predict when a bifurcation point has been reached. This critical moment marks the transition of a local incident into an irreversible, wide-ranging crisis, often fueled by authoritative sources or the strong emotional resonance of a message (Aboualola et al., 2023).

Furthermore, organizations must actively address the challenges of the infodemic and algorithmic amplification. Social media platforms' algorithms, which promote engaging content, inadvertently facilitate the rapid spread of disinformation, fake news, and even technically sophisticated deepfakes. Therefore, real-time management involves not only a rapid communication response (ideally within 15–30 minutes of escalation) but also the prompt implementation of fact-checking protocols and collaboration with platforms to limit the reach of false narratives. Actively neutralizing disinformation by engaging credible third parties is also essential, building greater credibility than relying solely on one's own statements (Kureyama et al., 2023).

Full preparedness and resilience are achieved through the establishment of a digital crisis command center (DCCC). This multidisciplinary unit transcends traditional PR structures by integrating legal, risk, operations, technical, and management into a single source of truth. The DCCC ensures consistent messaging across every digital channel and enables immediate decision-making, including legal liability assessment and prompt remediation to address the root cause of the crisis (Dadkhah et al., 2023).

Building digital trust through ethical and transparent crisis management remains a key element in this complex interaction. Organizations must avoid actions perceived as censorship (e.g., mass blocking of users) and instead employ communication segmentation, tailoring the tone and level of detail to specific stakeholder groups (customers, regulators, and investors). The ultimate goal is not only to minimize reputational damage but, above all, to transform the crisis experience into a process of continuous learning and regeneration, which is the essence of long-term organizational resilience (Kacperska et al., 2022).

Ultimately, resilience is not measured by the speed at which an organization extinguishes a fire but by the quality of relationships and the level of digital trust built before a crisis occurs. Real-time responses must be personalized for different stakeholder groups. Communication with regulators requires a different tone and level of detail than communication with business-to-consumer (B2C) customers, and yet another than communication with investors, even if all receive information via digital platforms. In the context of a social media crisis, organizations must adhere to the highest ethical standards and avoid aggressively deleting critical comments or blocking accounts, actions that are often interpreted as censorship and that lead to secondary escalation of the crisis (the so-called *Streisand effect*). Transparency, humility, and promptly accepting responsibility when warranted are fundamental to building digital trust (Mach, 2022).

In summary, real-time crisis management in the social media era has transformed from a PR function to a strategic operational capability. It is a continuous process of integrating people, technology (AI), and protocols (DCCC) to manage not only information but, above all, perception and trust in an environment where crises are inevitable and the only variable that can be controlled is the quality of the response.

Building trust and reputation as an element of resilience

Contemporary crisis management in the context of organizational resilience requires a fundamental shift in strategy from a reactive model to one of continuous anticipation and adaptation. The era of social media dominance has imposed a unique dual-track structure on crises, namely a cyber-physical dynamic in which content generated in the digital space immediately triggers measurable operational, legal, and financial impacts, forcing organizations to master real-time management. In this complex environment, strategically built digital trust and reputation are the foundations for both shock absorption and rapid recovery (Rust et al., 2021).

A key challenge in this dynamic is sensemaking, or the ability to quickly interpret the incomplete, chaotic, and often deliberately contradictory data that rapidly appears online. Effective resilience is demonstrated by integrating 24/7 monitoring systems with advanced linguistic analytics and AI, whose task is not only to track the volume of mentions but, above all, to identify weak signals and predict the bifurcation point—the critical moment when a local incident transforms into an irreversible crisis. This analytics must be fueled by continuous monitoring of reputational instability (reputational volatility), measured not only by current sentiment, but also by the Negative Emotional Engagement Index and Discourse Reciprocity, which allows the organization to track leading indicators of threat (Urquhart et al., 2025).

In the face of the algorithmic amplification of disinformation and fake news (infodemic), a solid reputation is the first line of defense. High levels of trust built during periods of stability create absorptive capital, providing the organization with "trustworthiness" in the initial phase of a crisis. Building digital trust rests on three pillars: transparency (proactive disclosure of information), consistency (a consistent tone and narrative across all platforms), and authenticity (an empathetic, human dialogue that connects the organization with stakeholders). Therefore, real-time management involves not only a rapid communication response but also the prompt implementation of fact-checking protocols and collaboration with platforms to limit the reach of false narratives, actively neutralizing them by engaging credible third parties (Sohaib & Han, 2023).

In the context of building brand trust in the digital world, in a study conducted by the authors (the study description is included in Chapter 2), respondents identified three main pillars essential for maintaining credibility and reputation. The most frequently cited element, noted by 75% of respondents, was transparency and honesty in communication. This dominant response is a key indicator of the growing importance of digital ethics, as in an era of disinformation and fake news, openness and truthfulness are perceived as the foundations of long-term reputation, directly building crisis resilience. The second most important element, indicated by 60% of companies, was the speed and quality of response (to inquiries or crises). The requirement for a near-instantaneous, professional, and empathetic response on social media platforms is perceived as a key element of operational resilience, minimizing potential reputational damage. The third factor, cited by 45% of respondents, was authenticity and consistency of message. Ensuring that a brand's messages align with its actual actions and values is a prerequisite for ensuring that they are not perceived as manipulation.

Trust is the core of digital responsibility. Respondents' emphasis on transparency (75%) and responsiveness (60%) as key pillars of trust confirms that digital responsibility is closely linked to ethical and open communication. In the context of the book, this conclusion is fundamental: companies build long-term resilience not only through technology and procedures but above all through ethical engagement with stakeholders, where integrity and responsiveness become measurable indicators of brand value.

Full preparedness and resilience are achieved through the establishment of a DCCC, which is more than just a communications team. It is a multidisciplinary unit that integrates legal, risk, operations, and management into a single source of truth. The DCCC ensures consistent messaging and enables immediate decision-making, which is essential for protecting and actively managing reputation as an external indicator of vitality. This strategy must be supported by digital leadership, where key decision-makers are visible and authentic, reinforcing the human element of resilience. Personal messages from leaders in crisis situations are perceived as significantly more credible, especially when they are aligned with the organization's publicly declared purpose-driven values (Radianti, 2021).

Ultimately, resilience is measured not by crisis avoidance but by the effectiveness of recovery, which is directly linked to the strength of the reputation built. In this phase, an organization must utilize social media as a public audit platform and feedback loop for adaptation. This involves public learning—informing about specific corrective actions implemented and actively integrating reputational insights into product and service optimization. This "public fixing" strategy closes the trust loop by visually documenting that public criticism has led to real improvements, transforming negative interaction into a positive benchmark for future sustainability. Overall, building trust and reputation is a dynamic strategy that embeds humility, transparency, and authenticity into the core of operational processes, treating each crisis as a trust test, the success of which determines long-term organizational resilience (Zhao et al., 2025).

Despite technological and strategic advancements in crisis management, organizational resilience is incomplete without taking into account a strict governance framework and the dynamic aspect of human decision-making in conditions of extreme stress. In a social media environment where information becomes public in a split second, a communication crisis immediately turns into a legal and regulatory risk. Trust and reputation are inextricably linked to compliance, and any online irregularity can be exploited in court proceedings or regulatory investigations. First, real-time management requires the implementation of UGC moderation mechanisms. Organizations are exposed to legal liability for tolerating violative content on their official channels—such as hate speech, defamation, or IP infringement. Therefore, crisis protocols must include guidelines for the immediate removal of such material while minimizing the risk of accusations of censorship, which requires transparency in moderation criteria. Second, a crisis often exposes gaps in compliance with global digital regulations. Regulations such as the European Digital Services Act (DSA) regarding transparency in algorithms and moderation, or the GDPR regarding user data management, provide frameworks that must be respected even in times of panic. Breaches in these areas, revealed during a crisis, multiply reputational damage. This makes systematic crisis data archiving—collecting all interactions, mentions, and decisions made on social media—a strategic imperative. This archiving, conducted legally and chronologically, is crucial for both auditing purposes and defending the organization in the event of potential legal disputes, transforming crisis data into defensive evidence (Hochstein et al., 2025)

Although technology aids detection and analysis, final decisions are made by humans under intense stress. Psychological resilience is therefore just as important as technological resilience. With the rapid development of a social media crisis, decision fatigue is a key threat to effectiveness. Time pressure leads to ill-considered, impulsive reactions that can deepen the crisis (e.g., aggressive or defensive communication and erroneous deletion of posts). To counteract this, crisis management must be equipped with clear pause points for key, high-level decisions and with automated processes for low-level activities, such as standard, lawyer-approved answers to frequently asked questions. This allows teams to maintain situational rationality (Fortes et al., 2021).

Moreover, building trust in a crisis requires understanding the psychology of reception. Social media audiences filter crisis messages through the prism of strong emotions: fear, anger, or a sense of betrayal. You can't just jump to facts and assurances. Effective communication must start with *Emotional Acknowledgment Validation*, i.e., expressing empathy and understanding stakeholder concerns before moving on to transparently presenting corrective actions. This sequence—Emotion, Empathy, Fact, and Action—is crucial for quickly rebuilding broken trust and is the ultimate test of digital leadership authenticity.

Integrating these dimensions—legal rigor and psychological awareness—strengthens organizational resilience, ensuring that a social media crisis is managed not only quickly but, above all, legally, ethically, and with respect for human capital.

Integration of social media data into decision-making processes

Contemporary organizational resilience management requires a fundamental transformation of the traditional approach to information. In the era of social media dominance, data from these platforms have ceased to be solely the domain of marketing and have become a key element feeding critical decision-making processes at the strategic, tactical, and operational levels. Full resilience requires systemic integration of social media data (social media data integration) as a factor enabling anticipation, rapid adaptation, and effective recovery. Consequently, social data integration becomes a fundamental requirement for effective sensemaking—that is, the organization's ability to interpret and make sense of unstructured signals from the environment. In the context of resilience, this data serves as early warning indicators, going beyond traditional reporting; it includes not only the identification of weak signals through volume and sentiment analysis but also reputational risk mapping, which precisely identifies key influencers or sources of disinformation. Incorporating these indicators into routine decision-making processes shortens detection time and increases the organization's absorption capital. Therefore, it is necessary to deepen analytics beyond simple sentiment. To achieve this, data integration must be based on an advanced topic modeling model, *which* groups discussions around specific vulnerabilities. Furthermore, for this data to be useful in cyber-physical crisis management, its geolocation and demographic analysis are essential (Hewapathirana, 2025).

Consequently, effective integration of social data requires its embedding in the DCCC and key departments, creating a horizontal decision-making architecture powered by social media data. At the strategic level (anticipation and governance), long-term data (e.g., evolving customer attitudes toward ESG) are integrated with management risk analysis; decisions about corporate policy revisions or supply chain restructuring are made based on social sentiment analysis. Then, at the tactical level (adaptation and communication), real-time data from monitoring tools determine the geography and demographics of the crisis's spread, and the decision to activate a fact-checking protocol is made based on analysis of the Discourse Reciprocity Index and source authority. Crucial in this phase is the use of NLP tools to distinguish between a joke/sarcasm and an actual complaint, allowing for proper communication segmentation.

Ultimately, at the operational level (response and recovery), direct feedback from social media must be automatically routed to ERP or CRM systems, which requires integration of technological application programming interfaces (APIs) with internal systems. Rapidly changing customer service procedures or recalling a defective product batch is the result of feedback loop integration; in this phase, social media data also serves to monitor the effectiveness of corrective actions, measuring how quickly sentiment returns to normal and how actively brand ambassadors support the recovery narrative. Despite these advanced benefits, data integration requires managing significant challenges to maintain resilience, including the need to extract factual information from informational noise and to maintain legal and ethical compliance, as tools must focus on aggregated sentiment rather than individual data and must strictly adhere to regulations such as the GDPR (Efunniyi et al., 2024).

Finally, organizational resilience must address the risks associated with platform dependency, as an organization does not control social media algorithms or privacy policies. Therefore, strategic decisions cannot be based solely on this data; integration requires cross-validation—combining social data with traditional data (e.g., customer surveys and sales reports), creating a hybrid decision-making model that minimizes one-sided risk and ensures the highest situational rationality in crisis management. In summary, integrating social media data into decision-making processes transforms organizational resilience from an abstract goal into a measurable operational capability. An organization that can transform network data streams into a single source of truth for its DCCC dramatically enhances its ability to adapt and maintain digital trust in the face of unpredictable crises.

Contemporary management within the framework of organizational resilience requires a fundamental transformation of the traditional approach to information. In the era of social media dominance, data from these platforms have ceased to be solely the domain of marketing and have become a key element feeding critical decision-making processes at the strategic, tactical, and operational levels. Full resilience requires systemic integration of social media data as a factor enabling anticipation, rapid adaptation, and effective recovery. Consequently, social data integration is becoming a fundamental requirement for effective sensemaking—that is, an organization's ability to interpret and assign meaning to unstructured signals from the environment. In the context of resilience, these data serve as early warning indicators, going beyond traditional reports. These include not only the identification of weak signals through volume and sentiment analysis but also reputational risk mapping, which precisely identifies key influencers or sources of disinformation. Incorporating these indicators into routine decision-making processes shortens threat detection time and increases an organization's absorption capital. Therefore, it is necessary to deepen analytics beyond simple sentiment. To achieve this, data integration must be based on an advanced topic modeling model. Furthermore, for this data to be useful in cyber-physical crisis management, its geolocation and demographic analysis are essential (Swaminathan et al., 2022).

Consequently, effective integration of social data requires its embedding in the DCCC and key departments, creating a horizontal decision-making architecture powered by social media data. At the strategic level (anticipation and governance), long-term data (e.g., evolving customer attitudes toward ESG) is integrated with management risk analysis; decisions about corporate policy revisions or supply chain restructuring are made based on social sentiment analysis. Then, at the tactical level (adaptation and communication), real-time data from monitoring tools determine the geography and demographics of the crisis's spread, and the decision to activate a fact-checking protocol is made based on analysis of the Discourse Reciprocity Index and source authority. Crucial in this phase is the use of NLP tools to distinguish between a joke/sarcasm and an actual complaint, allowing for proper communication segmentation (Kumar & Gupta, 2023).

Ultimately, at the operational level (response and recovery), direct feedback from social media must be automatically routed to ERP or CRM systems, which requires technological API integration with internal systems. Rapidly changing customer service procedures or recalling a defective product batch is the result of feedback loop integration; in this phase, social media data are also used to monitor the effectiveness of corrective actions, measuring how quickly sentiment returns to normal. Despite these advanced benefits, data integration requires managing significant challenges to maintain resilience, including maintaining legal and ethical compliance and managing informational noise. Finally, organizational resilience must address the risks associated with platform dependency; hence, integration requires cross-validation: comparing social data with traditional data to create a hybrid decision-making model.

Market practice confirms the crucial importance of this horizontal decision-making approach. The study conducted by the authors (described in Chapter 2) reveals a varied but significant level of integration of social media data analysis into decision-making processes. Data are used to a fully integrated level (5) by 30% of companies. These are digital leaders who utilize advanced social media tools. Listening is not only used in marketing but also in strategic product development and business model reconfiguration. Another 35% rate integration as "high" (4). This group, representing the majority of large companies, regularly uses social media data to evaluate campaigns, identify market trends, and obtain direct product feedback. A total of 65% of respondents indicated high or full integration, demonstrating the growing importance of a data-driven approach in managing large-scale organizations and, consequently, building resilience through the ability to quickly diagnose the market environment. This contrasts with 20% of companies who rate integration as "moderate" (3) and the smallest percentage (15%) declaring a low level of integration (1–2), which is characteristic of entities with limited strategic awareness.

Despite such advanced benefits, data integration requires managing significant challenges to maintain resilience, including maintaining legal and ethical compliance and managing informational noise. Finally, organizational resilience must address the risks associated with platform dependency; hence, integration requires cross-validation: combining social data with traditional data to create a hybrid decision-making model that minimizes one-sided risk (Enarsson et al., 2022).

For the entire data- and trust-based crisis management architecture to make business sense, rigorous auditing and measurement of the ROI in digital resilience is essential. In this context, digital trust must be quantified, as the loss of reputation on social media translates into measurable reputational crisis costs, such as a decline in stock value, higher CAC, or the loss of top talent. Resilience is therefore an investment that minimizes these losses. Management must move from traditional KPIs to key resilience indicators (KRIs), which focus on the ability to anticipate and adapt. Key KRIs powered by social media data include mean time to detect (MTTD)—the average time it takes to detect a weak signal on social media; mean time to respond/resolve (MTTR)—the average time from detection to the first message or implementation of a corrective action; and Sentiment Recovery Index—the time it takes for sentiment to return to pre-crisis levels. Furthermore, resilience requires a periodic review of procedures; the integration of social media data is crucial in crisis simulations (tabletop exercises), where the DCCC's responsiveness is tested based on realistic crisis scenarios generated from dynamic network data. This approach ensures that data integration is not an end in itself but a tool for minimizing financial and strategic risk, thus closing the loop of continuous improvement and investment in long-term sustainability (Kolajo et al., 2022).

However, no metrics or procedures can replace the human factor. This requires a strategic investment in digital literacy and organizational culture. It's essential to shift from a culture of "avoiding mistakes" to one of "learning from mistakes quickly and transparently", which is the essence of social media resilience. This is achieved through multilevel training not only for the DCCC team but also for management (digital leadership) and front-line employees, ensuring everyone understands their role in quickly detecting and escalating crisis signals.

Looking to the future, digital resilience will be increasingly supported by future technologies. We can expect blockchain technology to be used to digitally verify the authenticity of messages and identities, which is a direct response to the threat of deepfakes and disinformation. Furthermore, generative AI will find applications in crisis simulations (tabletop exercises), creating an infinite number of realistic and dynamic scenarios modeled on network data, thereby increasing anticipatory capacity on an unprecedented scale. This approach ensures that data integration is not an end in itself but a tool for minimizing financial and strategic risk, thereby closing the loop of continuous improvement and investment in people and innovation, which ultimately guarantee long-term sustainability.

References

Aboualola, M., Abualsaud, K., Khattab, T., Zorba, N., & Hassanein, H. S. (2023). Edge technologies for disaster management: A survey of social media and artificial intelligence integration. *IEEE Access*, *11*, 73782–73802.

Aïmeur, E., Amri, S., & Brassard, G. (2023). Fake news, disinformation and misinformation in social media: A review. *Social Network Analysis and Mining*, *13*(1), 30.

Chen, J., & Liu, L. (2025). Social media usage for service innovation: A resilience perspective. *The Service Industries Journal*, *45*(5–6), 582–603.

Dadkhah, S., Zhang, X., Weismann, A. G., Firouzi, A., & Ghorbani, A. A. (2023). The largest social media ground-truth dataset for real/fake content: Truthseeker. *IEEE Transactions on Computational Social Systems*, *11*(3), 3376–3390.

Efunniyi, C. P., Abhulimen, A. O., Obiki-Osafiele, A. N., Osundare, O. S., Agu, E. E., & Adeniran, I. A. (2024). Strengthening corporate governance and financial compliance: Enhancing accountability and transparency. *Finance & Accounting Research Journal*, *6*(8), 1597–1616.

Enarsson, T., Enqvist, L., & Naarttijärvi, M. (2022). Approaching the human in the loop–legal perspectives on hybrid human/algorithmic decision-making in three contexts. *Information & Communications Technology Law*, *31*(1), 123–153.

Fortes, L. S., Fonseca, F. S., Nakamura, F. Y., Barbosa, B. T., Gantois, P., de Lima-Júnior, D., & Ferreira, M. E. (2021). Effects of mental fatigue induced by social media use on volleyball decision-making, endurance, and countermovement jump performance. *Perceptual and Motor Skills*, *128*(6), 2745–2766.

Hewapathirana, I. U. (2025). Advancing tourism demand forecasting in Sri Lanka: Evaluating the performance of machine learning models and the impact of social media data integration. *Journal of Tourism Futures*, *11*(2), 261–285.

Hochstein, R. E., Harmeling, C. M., & Perko, T. (2025). Toward a theory of consumer digital trust: Meta-analytic evidence of its role in the effectiveness of user-generated content. *Journal of the Academy of Marketing Science*, *53*(4), 1034–1054.

Kacperska, E., Łukasiewicz, K., & Horin, N. (2022). Building digital trust in social media during crisis. In *Trust, digital business and technology* (pp. 49–60). Routledge.

Kolajo, T., Daramola, O., & Adebiyi, A. A. (2022). Real-time event detection in social media streams through semantic analysis of noise terms. *Journal of Big Data*, *9*(1), 90.

Kumar, A. M., & Gupta, S. (2023). Governance of social media platforms: A literature review. *Pacific Asia Journal of the Association for Information Systems*, *15*(1), 3.

Kureyama, N., Terada, M., Kusudo, M., Nozawa, K., Wanifuchi-Endo, Y., Fujita, T., Asano, T., Kato, A., Mori, M., Horisawa, N., & Toyama, T. (2023). Fact-checking cancer information on social media in Japan: Retrospective study using Twitter. *JMIR Formative Research*, *7*(1), e49452.

Mach, M. (2022). Streisand effect in the context of the right to be forgotten. *European Studies-The Review of European Law, Economics and Politics*, *9*(1), 110–121.

Martín-Rojas, R., Garrido-Moreno, A., & García-Morales, V. J. (2023). Social media use, corporate entrepreneurship and organizational resilience: A recipe for SMEs success in a post-Covid scenario. *Technological Forecasting and Social Change*, *190*, 122421.

Radianti, J. (2021). Experimental command and control center for crisis and disaster management: A living-lab approach. In *Emerging technologies for disaster resilience: Practical cases and theories* (pp. 201–227). Springer Singapore.

Rammane, M., Mesmoudi, S., Tri, A., Braikat, B., & Damil, N. (2021). Bifurcation points and bifurcated branches in fluids mechanics by high-order meshfree geometric progression algorithms. *International Journal for Numericals Methods in Fluids*, *93*(3), 834–852.

Rust, R. T., Rand, W., Huang, M. H., Stephen, A. T., Brooks, G., & Chabuk, T. (2021). Real-time brand reputation tracking using social media. *Journal of Marketing*, *85*(4), 21–43.

Sohaib, M., & Han, H. (2023). Building value co-creation with social media marketing, brand trust, and brand loyalty. *Journal of Retailing and Consumer Services*, *74*, 103442.

Swaminathan, V., Schwartz, H. A., Menezes, R., & Hill, S. (2022). The language of brands in social media: Using topic modeling on social media conversations to drive brand strategy. *Journal of Interactive Marketing*, *57*(2), 255–277.

Urquhart, C., Cheuk, B., Lam, L., & Snowden, D. (2025). Sense-making, sensemaking and sense making – A systematic review and meta-synthesis of literature in information science and education: An annual review of information science and technology (ARIST) paper. *Journal of the Association for Information Science and Technology*, *76*(1), 3–97.

Zhao, X., Yu, F., Zhang, X., Chen, J., & Li, P. (2025). Assessing urban renewal efficiency via multi-source data and DID-based comparison between historical districts. *npj Heritage Science*, *13*(1), 389.

5 Ethical and social aspects of management in the digital environment

Privacy, data, and transparency in user relations

Contemporary management in a dynamic digital environment is undergoing a fundamental transformation in which data has become not only the most valuable strategic asset of enterprises but also a major flashpoint in ethical debates. In the era of the data-driven economy, organizations constantly collect, process, and monetize information about the identities, behaviors, and preferences of their users, redefining the traditional understanding of market relations. This process, while driving innovation and enabling unprecedented personalization of services, also raises profound dilemmas regarding the limits of corporate interference in individual private lives. In this context, privacy is no longer perceived merely as a technical aspect of cybersecurity but rather a crucial human right, which, when confronted with aggressive business models such as surveillance capitalism, is systematically eroded. Managers today face the difficult challenge of managing growing information asymmetry, where users are often unaware of the true scale or purpose of their digital footprint. As a consequence, the transparency of corporate activities becomes a scarce value, often obscured by complicated regulations and opaque AI algorithms, functioning as "black boxes" incomprehensible to the consumer (Zhang et al., 2022).

A lack of transparency in user communication leads to a serious crisis of trust, which in the long term can threaten the stability and reputation of even the largest organizations. Managerial responsibility therefore extends far beyond formal compliance with legal regulations such as the GDPR, requiring the adoption of a proactive digital ethics approach. Ethical management in this area must eliminate the use of so-called dark design patterns that manipulate consumer decision-making processes and instead adopt solutions that truly respect user autonomy. The concept of CSR is evolving toward corporate digital responsibility (CDR), in which data protection is treated as a social obligation rather than merely a bureaucratic requirement. Companies that can implement privacy-conscious design principles and ensure a fair exchange of values build a more sustainable competitive advantage based on loyalty. It is important to note that users are increasingly faced with the dilemma of choosing between

DOI: 10.4324/9781003730507-6

digital convenience and the protection of their private sphere, which imposes an additional educational burden on service providers. These issues are inextricably linked to the problem of algorithmic justice and the risk of discrimination, making data management a deeply sociological issue. Modern leaders must therefore balance the pursuit of data profit maximization with the imperative of protecting human dignity online. Ultimately, how organizations approach the triad of values— privacy, data, and transparency—will determine the shape of the future information society and the place of humans in an automated world (Lipschultz, 2023).

Referring to the authors' research (described in Chapter 2) regarding how they ensure transparency regarding the use of user data, the dominant response indicates moderate transparency (50%). These companies comply with minimum legal requirements (e.g., GDPR) but do not take additional steps to simplify and communicate complex analytical processes, including algorithmic operation. Full transparency was declared by 30% of respondents. These are organizations that treat data transparency as a strategic competitive advantage, actively simplifying communication about algorithms and processes. A total of 80% of companies have achieved a satisfactory level of transparency. The remaining 20% of companies that provide limited or no transparency limit themselves to the absolute minimum required by law or struggle to fully implement transparency principles. The dominance of the legal compliance model over the strategic transparency model is clear.

The foundation of the contemporary digital economy has been a paradigmatic shift in the perception of data, which has evolved from an ancillary resource into a key strategic asset, often referred to as the "new currency" or "21st-century oil". At the heart of this ecosystem are business models that redefine traditional market exchange, basing their profitability not on the direct sale of products or services but on the monetization of information obtained from users. The dominant mechanism in this area is the so-called zero-price model, in which advanced digital tools—from search engines to social media to navigation maps—are made available to consumers free of charge. In reality, however, this transaction is essentially barter, where the hidden but extremely expensive currency is user privacy and the right to insight into their behavior. This phenomenon raises fundamental ethical questions about the transparency of the value of this exchange, as the average consumer is rarely able to estimate the true market value of the data they provide to corporations in exchange for free access to applications (Yang & Ge, 2022).

A deeper analysis of this mechanism leads to the concept of "surveillance capitalism", popularized in academic discourse, which describes the process of unilaterally appropriating human experience as a free resource. In this approach, data is not merely a record of the user's actions but is used to generate so-called behavioral surplus. AI-based management systems analyze this information not only to improve services, which would be ethically justified, but above all to create predictive products. These products, sold on digital advertising futures markets, are used to predict and, in extreme cases, modify future consumer behavior. The ethical burden of this business model lies in the objectification of the user; the user ceases to be an autonomous customer whose favor is courted and becomes an object of extraction, whose choices are cataloged, profiled, and sold to third parties without full and informed consent (Montag & Elhai, 2023).

As a result, a drastic asymmetry of information and power in the company-customer relationship is emerging. Digital organizations possess almost unlimited knowledge about intimate aspects of individuals' lives, while the mechanisms of their algorithms remain opaque "black boxes". This balance of power creates the risk of manipulation on an unprecedented scale, exploiting users' psychological vulnerabilities to maximize time spent on platforms (the attention economy) and increase advertising conversions. From a management ethics perspective, persisting with business models that fundamentally contradict the right to privacy and individual autonomy is becoming increasingly risky. The challenge for contemporary managers, therefore, is to find alternative ways of generating revenue that shift away from invasive data exploitation toward subscription models or those in which users participate in the profits from their own data, thus restoring subjectivity in digital relationships.

In user-organization relationships, the digital interface (user interface) has ceased to be a neutral medium and has become a key tool for shaping consumer decisions, which gives user experience (UX) design a profound ethical dimension. From a management perspective, the presentation of privacy information is no longer just a matter of esthetics or functionality but an element of a "choice architecture" that can support individual autonomy or systemically limit it. A central ethical issue in this area is the widespread use of so-called dark web browsers. Dark patterns are design strategies that deliberately exploit cognitive biases and heuristics of human thinking to induce users to take actions they would not consciously undertake, such as consenting to tracking or subscribing to unwanted services (Avalle et al., 2024). Designers, often operating under pressure from business metrics (KPIs), create interfaces in which pro-privacy options are hidden, visually devalued, or difficult to access, while consent to data sharing is implicit and presented as the only intuitive path. Such a practice, while often bordering on legality, fundamentally violates the principle of customer loyalty, turning trust into an exploitable resource.

In parallel with the problem of visual manipulation, there is the phenomenon of illusory consent, resulting from information overload and the complexity of decision-making processes. The current "notice and consent" model, materializing in the form of ubiquitous cookie banners, has led to so-called consent fatigue. Users, bombarded with dozens of requests daily, fall into automaticity, clicking acceptance buttons without reflection, making the consent process a formality devoid of ethical content. Managers must therefore face the fact that consent forced by an irritating or confusing interface is not informed consent. Furthermore, this problem is exacerbated by the hermetic language of terms and conditions and privacy policies, which, instead of serving a communicative function, have become legal shields for corporations. The extreme asymmetry of knowledge between service providers and recipients, perpetuated by incomprehensible legal jargon, prevents consumers from rationally assessing the risks associated with sharing data (Hanlon & Jones, 2023).

In response to these challenges, ethical management in the digital environment requires a fundamental shift in the design paradigm—a shift from concealing intentions to radical transparency. This means implementing solutions in which information about data processing is provided in a layered, contextual, and understandable way through "just-in-time" notices, delivered exactly at the moment when the user makes a decision (Shahidzadeh & Shokouhyar, 2024).

True transparency in UX isn't about providing thousands of pages of legal documentation but rather about visualizing data flow and the consequences of choices in a way that's accessible to the layman. Companies that decide to eliminate deceptive interfaces and invest in usable privacy treat transparency not as a barrier to conversion but as an investment in the long-term credibility of the brand and anticipate upcoming legal regulations that increasingly judge manipulative design practices (Malkin, 2022).

The issue of interface transparency and consent mechanisms is merely the surface layer of the ethical challenges of digital governance, serving as a mere visual manifestation of processes occurring deep within IT systems. A natural consequence of analyzing how users interact overtly with applications is therefore the need to delve into the invisible mechanisms that control these interactions and give meaning to the collected data. While manipulative design (UX) influences what users do, algorithms and AI determine how users are perceived, classified, and treated by the organization, shifting the burden of managerial responsibility to the level of decision-making architecture.

Here we return to the area of trust management in the era of so-called black box algorithms. A central ethical dilemma is the fact that key decisions affecting customers' life chances—from creditworthiness assessments, through insurance pricing, to recruitment qualifications—are delegated to AI systems whose operating logic often remains impenetrable even to their creators. This technological opacity creates a serious risk of algorithmic discrimination. Because ML models are trained on historical datasets, they inevitably inherit the human biases and stereotypes contained within them. Without proper managerial oversight, automated systems can unwittingly replicate and even reinforce social inequalities on a massive scale, categorizing users according to sensitive characteristics in ways that would be considered illegal or unethical in an analog world (Cotter, 2023).

An equally important aspect is the use of advanced analytics to predict and modify behavior through microtargeting. By analyzing thousands of data points, algorithms can identify moments of emotional vulnerability in users, blurring the line between beneficial personalization of offers and ruthless manipulation of individual vulnerabilities. In this context, ethical management requires a shift from blind faith in the infallibility of technology to implementing the concept of explainable AI (XAI). Organizations must be ready not only to utilize the results of algorithmic operation but also to explain to the customer—in understandable language—why a specific decision has been made. Managerial responsibility in the digital environment is therefore evolving toward the role of an ethical auditor, who must ensure that the pursuit of optimization and algorithmic efficiency does not come at the expense of social justice and human agency (Gong et al., 2024).

In response to the identified challenges of aggressive business models, manipulative interfaces, and algorithmic opacity, the focus is shifting to the strategic level, where privacy protection and data ethics are no longer the exclusive domain of legal or IT departments but are increasingly regarded as strategic imperatives for top management. Effectively addressing these issues requires a fundamental shift in organizational culture, with the concept of CSR evolving into CDR. In this approach, ethical data management is treated not as a costly regulatory requirement but as a key factor in building a competitive advantage based on trust. This strategy assumes a shift from reactive "firefighting" in the event of a data breach to a proactive approach, based on the principle of privacy by design and default. This means that user privacy protection is considered from the conceptual stage of product or service development, becoming an integral part of the system architecture, not just an additional security overlay (Herden et al., 2021). Implementing this strategy in managerial practice involves rigorous adherence to the principle of data minimization. Organizations must abandon the previously dominant "Big-data" philosophy, which involves collecting all possible information "just in case", in favor of a "smart data" approach, which collects only the data necessary to achieve a specific business goal. Instead of being an asset, excess data becomes a "toxic resource", increasing risk and potential reputational damage in the event of a security breach.

An equally important element of the strategy is managing transparency in crisis situations. A modern managerial approach to security incidents (data breach) rejects the tactic of concealing problems from the public. Instead, it promotes open communication, in which the company immediately informs users of the threat, accepts responsibility, and presents a remediation plan. This approach, while damaging to the brand's image in the short term, helps maintain the brand's credibility in the eyes of stakeholders in the long term. Ultimately, an organization's digital maturity is measured not only by the technological advancement of its algorithms but, above all, by its ability to self-regulate and its willingness to prioritize the well-being of digital users over short-term profits, which will be the key determinant of market leadership in the future economy (Bachura et al., 2022).

Organizational responsibility for content, disinformation, and moderation

Expanding the ethical discourse beyond the sphere of data acquisition and protection, it is necessary to pay attention to the second pillar of digital responsibility, which is the way organizations manage the information they distribute. While in the previous approach the user was a passive source of data, in the context of content the user becomes an active recipient and creator, which shifts the burden of managerial responsibility from protecting privacy to protecting the quality of public debate and cognitive security. Modern digital platforms, for years positioning themselves as neutral technological intermediaries (mere conduits) are now faced with the need to redefine their identity, recognizing that algorithmic content selection makes them de facto powerful curators of social reality. This "platform neutrality" paradigm ultimately collapsed in the face of the realities of the attention economy, where recommendation algorithms, focused on maximizing engagement, systematically promote sensational, extreme, and polarizing content, deeming it the most effective in keeping users glued to their screens. Managers are therefore faced with a dilemma: should they optimize business metrics (KPIs) at the expense of the health of the social fabric, or should they undertake ethical intervention in the flow of information?

A direct consequence of algorithmic favoring of emotional content is the vulnerability of digital ecosystems to disinformation and influence operations. Organizations managing social media and content aggregators are becoming unwitting, and sometimes complicit, actors in the processes of destabilizing democracy and eroding social trust. Organizational responsibility in this area requires the implementation of advanced fact-checking mechanisms and strategies to combat so-called deepfakes—synthetic media generated by AI that blur the line between truth and falsehood. Reputational risk management is inextricably linked to civic ethics; a company that allows the uncontrolled spread of conspiracy theories or hate speech risks not only regulatory sanctions (such as the EU DSA) but also a boycott from informed consumers and advertisers (brand). The challenge for leaders is therefore to create systems that are resistant to manipulation but that do not fall into the trap of arbitrary censorship, which requires transparent definition of community standards (Saurwein & Spencer-Smith, 2021).

Enforcing these standards raises the issue of content moderation, one of the most complex operational and ethical issues in digital governance. This process, often invisible to the average user, relies on the hybrid collaboration of automated AI filters and the work of thousands of human moderators. This is where the dark side of digital HR management becomes apparent: these workers, often outsourced to developing countries, are exposed daily to graphic content (violence and child pornography), leading to serious mental health issues, including post-traumatic stress disorder (PTSD). Managers' ethical responsibility requires providing these workers with adequate psychological support, decent pay, and job rotation, rather than treating them as interchangeable cogs in an Internet-cleaning machine. On the other hand, relying solely on automated AI moderation risks contextual errors and the removal of legal content, which can be perceived as restricting freedom of expression (Gull et al., 2023).

Ultimately, content management and moderation boils down to a fundamental question about corporate power over public discourse (governance). In the absence of universal definitions of "hate speech" or "disinformation", private companies are taking on the role of arbiters of truth, which raises concerns about the legitimacy of their decisions. A modern approach to governance in this area involves the creation of external supervisory boards (oversight boards), auditing algorithms by independent entities, and publishing detailed transparency reports that explain the scale and reasons for content removal. Organizational accountability is therefore evolving toward a co-management model, in which the company opens its decision-making processes to social and academic scrutiny. Managers of the future must possess not only technological but also sociological competencies to efficiently navigate between the obligation to ensure user safety and respect for their fundamental right to free speech, knowing that every moderation decision has a real impact on shaping public opinion in the real world (Saniuk & Grabowska, 2022).

Continuing the empirical analysis based on the authors' research on digital responsibility and ethics, the results indicate that when asked about the level of activity aimed at countering disinformation and moderating content on company channels, 35% of respondents reported being highly engaged. This group comprises large companies with strong digital responsibility that have formal moderation policies and actively monitor disinformation. Another 40% of respondents declared active engagement. These are large companies conducting regular and active moderation, responding to false or harmful content. A total of 75% of the surveyed companies therefore have an active strategy in this area, demonstrating an understanding that digital hygiene is an integral part of reputation management. Only 15% rated their activities as moderate, suggesting a reactive approach (based on reports) rather than proactive fact-checking. The smallest group, representing 10% of companies, demonstrates little or no involvement, which is most often due to limited resources for professional moderation.

The results of the analysis of ethics and digital responsibility confirm the growing strategic maturity of large enterprises but at the same time highlight a clear differentiation in the scope of proactive actions necessary to build organizational resilience.

First, organizational content responsibility is taken seriously: a total of 75% of respondents engage in active or very active counteracting and moderation of disinformation, demonstrating an understanding that digital hygiene is an integral part of reputation management. However, the challenge lies in shifting from reactive (report-based) actions to proactive fact-checking, which still poses a barrier for smaller entities. Second, in the area of data transparency and privacy, companies have achieved a satisfactory level of compliance, with 80% of them declaring full or moderate transparency. However, the "legal compliance" model (50% moderate) dominates, meaning the challenge is to transform transparency from a requirement into a strategic competitive advantage, requiring simplified communication about complex algorithms and analytical processes. Third, the area of inclusivity and equal access remains the most heterogeneous, with 55% of companies only partially implementing this practice. This suggests that while large corporations fully integrate diversity and inclusion (D&I) principles (30% "yes"), for most medium-sized and small companies, inclusivity remains an aspirational goal rather than a fully formalized and consistently implemented digital strategy.

All these findings lead to the conclusion that digital responsibility is a key, yet still unevenly implemented, pillar that is necessary for building sustainable organizational resilience, with the greatest gaps visible in the transition from minimal legal compliance to strategic proactivity.

The operationalization of content responsibility in digital ecosystems requires managers to make strategic decisions about the balance between technological efficiency and human sensitivity, which manifests itself in the dilemma of choosing between algorithmic moderation and manual review. AI-based systems have become the first line of defense in the fight against the deluge of harmful information, offering scalability and responsiveness unattainable by humans. In an environment where thousands of hours of video and millions of posts are generated every minute, only automated filters can identify and block clearly illegal content in real time, such as spam, malware, or known child abuse images (via hashing mechanisms). From a management perspective, AI also ensures the desired consistency of decisions in simple cases and 24/7 availability, which is crucial for global platforms operating across multiple time zones. However, this technological efficiency carries a significant ethical risk in the form of so-called context blindness; despite advances in NLP, algorithms still struggle to distinguish hate speech from educational citations, satire from disinformation, and nudity in art from pornography. This leads to over-blocking, which can be perceived as unjustified censorship and a violation of users' freedom of speech, thus generating reputational risk for the platform (Just & Saurwein, 2024).

In response to these limitations, a human factor becomes a necessary complement to the process, bringing to moderation a rudimentary ability to understand cultural nuances, authorial intentions, and the specifics of local social conflicts. Human moderators serve as the final arbiters in so-called gray areas, where assessing the harmfulness of content is ambiguous and requires empathy and deeper semantic analysis, which a machine cannot perform. However, managers must consider that manual moderation is a costly, slow, and difficult-to-scale process during sudden viral crises. Furthermore, it introduces an element of subjectivity, as moderators' decisions may be biased by their own biases or cultural background, leading to inconsistent enforcement of rules. However, the greatest ethical challenge in managing human teams remains the aforementioned psychological cost discussed earlier, as this work involves constant exposure to digital evil, which imposes a moral obligation on the employer to provide an extensive wellness support system and job rotation to prevent burnout and trauma (Choli & Kuss, 2021).

The optimal management model emerging from this analysis is a hybrid human-in-the- loop approach. In this strategy, AI acts as a coarse sieve, filtering out obvious content and prioritizing reports, while humans handle cases requiring value judgment and reviewing user appeals. This synergy mitigates the shortcomings of both solutions: AI increases human efficiency by protecting them from some of the most graphic content, while humans correct the cognitive biases of machines by teaching algorithms to better recognize new threats. Managing this process, however, requires constant transparency; the organization must clearly communicate to users when decisions were made by machines and when they were made by humans, and it must provide a viable appeals process. Ultimately, technology in content moderation should be treated as a tool supporting human judgment, not a mechanism that absolves managers of moral responsibility for the shape of public debate on their platforms (Zhou et al., 2024).

Equality of access and inclusivity in digital management

Expanding the ethical horizon of management in the digital environment beyond the issues of privacy and content control, we should consider the fundamental issue of distributive justice, that is, equal access to digital resources and inclusiveness in their design. In modern managerial discourse, the problem of digital exclusion, the so-called "divide", is no longer perceived in binary terms—as a simple division between those with and without access to the Internet. Managers now face second- and third-degree exclusion, which concerns, respectively, the lack of digital skills necessary to effectively use tools and the disparity in the benefits that different social groups derive from being online. Organizational responsibility in this regard means designing digital strategies that do not favor users with the latest equipment and fast broadband connections, which is particularly important in the context of global expansion into markets with weaker infrastructure (Global South). Ignoring the technical and competency limitations of segments of the population leads to so-called technological elitism, in which digital services, instead of democratizing access to goods, become a barrier that deepens social stratification (Lybeck et al., 2024).

An integral element of ethical management is the accessibility paradigm, often abbreviated as a11y (A-eleven-Y). It goes far beyond the legal obligation to adapt websites to Web Content Accessibility Guidelines (WCAG) standards for people with disabilities. From a management perspective, accessibility becomes a driver of innovation, in line with the concept of the "curb-cut effect"—solutions designed with excluded groups in mind (e.g., video captions for the deaf) ultimately benefit society as a whole (e.g., people watching content in noisy environments). Product managers who fail to consider an inclusive perspective during prototyping risk creating solutions that systemically discriminate against seniors, neuroatypical individuals, or users with different perception patterns. Ethics in this dimension dictates a shift from designing for the statistical "average user"—who, in reality, does not exist—to universal design that considers the full spectrum of human diversity (Sharma et al., 2024).

The internal dimension of inclusiveness in digital management is revealed in the new model of hybrid and remote work, which creates the risk of the so-called "proximity bias". This is a psychological phenomenon in which managers unconsciously favor employees they physically see in the office, assigning them higher competencies and offering them more promotions, at the expense of remote workers. Since remote work is more often chosen by women, caregivers of dependents, and people with disabilities, uncontrolled "proximity bias" can lead to regression in terms of managerial diversity and the re-creation of glass ceilings in virtual structures. Ethical leadership in the digital era therefore requires the implementation of deliberate employee evaluation procedures based solely on measurable results, a principle known as output-based management, rather than on physical presence, and the assurance of equal access to informal knowledge networks within the organization, regardless of employee's location (Hong et al., 2024).

Ultimately, the issue of inclusivity touches on the very epistemology of technology creation—who decides the shape of digital reality. The homogeneity of development and management teams (often dominated by a single demographic) leads to the creation of products burdened by "cultural blindness". If marginalized groups are not represented in the decision-making process, their needs and threats are systematically overlooked not out of malice but rather due to a lack of awareness. Examples include facial recognition systems that are less effective at recognizing darker complexions, or voice assistants that lack understanding of local dialects. Therefore, building diverse teams (DI) in the technology sector is not merely a PR or HR requirement but a fundamental ethical and qualitative requirement. Only an inclusive creative process can ensure that the final digital solutions serve the entire society equitably, minimizing the risk of technology becoming a tool for new segregation.

In order to consolidate the theoretical assumptions of ethical management in the digital environment, it is crucial to refer to specific, high-profile cases illustrating the scale of problems at the intersection of technology, business, and society. The conflict begins with a fundamental dispute over the business model, exemplified by the clash between Apple and Meta (Facebook) over tracking transparency under Apple's ATT framework. Apple positions privacy as a premium feature of its hardware, effectively hindering tracking in apps, while Meta, which relies on an advertising model, has reported billions in losses. This conflict has exposed not only the asymmetry of power in the technology market but also the fragility of business models based on secret data extraction. Moreover, this fight for data descends to the level of interaction with the consumer, where deliberate manipulation is used; Amazon's "Iliad" project has become a textbook example of so-called dark patterns, in which the Prime subscription cancellation process was deliberately complicated to discourage users from making decisions that were unfavorable to the company. From a managerial perspective, these cases provide evidence that short-sighted optimization of retention rates using manipulative design equates to legal risk and loss of trust (Reiberg, 2022).

Moving from the problem of manipulation at the interface level to the automation of decision-making processes, systemic algorithmic bias becomes an equally glaring threat. This was revealed in Amazon's internal recruiting tool, which automatically discriminated against female candidates based on historically male-dominated data. This problem has also spilled over into the financial sphere, as evidenced by the Apple Card case (Goldman Sachs), where an algorithm granted women lower credit limits than their husbands, despite having equivalent creditworthiness. In both cases, intentional discrimination was not proven but the inability of decision-makers to explain the logic behind the AI's "black box" operation created an ethical and legal crisis, demonstrating that automation without an ethical audit of training data can lead to the reproduction of biases on an industrial scale.

While algorithmic bias generates economic harm for individuals, another category of problems concerns digital platforms in their role as curators of public debate, where poor moderation has global social consequences. A particularly tragic example is the role of the Meta platform (Facebook) in the genocide of the Rohingya minority in Myanmar. Despite repeated warnings, the company failed to invest in effective Burmese-language moderation, allowing hate speech and incitement to violence to spread, which a United Nations (UN) report identified as a decisive factor in the escalation of the conflict. Furthermore, in the political sphere, the threat of disinformation has materialized in deepfakes, exemplified by a fake video of the Ukrainian president calling for surrender, which places the imperative on media managers to defend information integrity in an environment increasingly susceptible to real-time manipulation.

Ultimately, all these issues—from privacy to disinformation—pale in comparison to the fundamental lack of digital equity and inclusivity. This issue gained legal prominence in the high-profile case of Domino's Pizza versus Guillermo Robles, in which the court ruled that the website and mobile app of a pizzeria chain must be fully accessible to people with disabilities, in accordance with the accessibility principles. This decision established that digital services are subject to the same inclusiveness requirements as physical spaces, making accessibility management not only an ethical postulate but also a strict legal requirement. This phenomenon complements the internal problem: in remote and hybrid work environments, "proximity bias" is increasingly prevalent, complementing the organization's internal challenges. This bias occurs when managers unconsciously favor employees who are physically present in the office. This bias, leading to unfair promotion distribution, poses a serious ethical risk to management inclusivity. Together, these cases demonstrate that managing in the digital age requires a holistic perspective, where every issue—from recruitment algorithms to website accessibility—is essentially an ethical issue with real business and societal consequences (Kollnig et al., 2022).

Contemporary management in the digital environment faces a critical ethical imperative stemming from the role of data as a key strategic asset. The entire analysis reveals that market success is inextricably linked to social responsibility, which compels organizations to adopt a proactive CDR approach and implement the privacy by design principle, breaking away from business models based on predatory and covert monetization of information. Key operational dilemmas revolve around combating consumer manipulation through dark patterns. Patterns in user interfaces, and systemic injustice generated by opaque, historically biased algorithms (the black box). This phenomenon, combined with the problem of disinformation and the need to scale content moderation, shifts responsibility for the quality of public debate and real social harm to managers, placing them in the role of arbiters between freedom of speech and security. Furthermore, the ethical dimension of management encompasses combating digital exclusion at all levels, requiring investment in equal access and inclusive design that treats accessibility as a business requirement, not merely a marginal legal obligation (Mazhar & Dwivedi, 2024). Ultimately, the effectiveness of a modern leader is measured not only by technological efficiency but above all by the ability to strategically balance profit with social justice, moving from minimal legal compliance to maximum moral commitment to building trust and digital inclusivity.

References

Avalle, M., Di Marco, N., Etta, G., Sangiorgio, E., Alipour, S., Bonetti, A., Alvisi, L., Scala, A., Baronchelli, A., Cinelli, M., & Quattrociocchi, W. (2024). Persistent interaction patterns across social media platforms and over time. *Nature*, *628*(8008), 582–589.

Bachura, E., Valecha, R., Chen, R., & Rao, H. R. (2022). The OPM data breach: An investigation of shared emotional reactions on Twitter. *MIS Quarterly*, *46*(2), 881–910.

Choli, M., & Kuss, D. J. (2021). Perceptions of blame on social media during the coronavirus pandemic. *Computers in Human Behavior*, *124*, 106895.

Cotter, K. (2023). "Shadowbanning is not a thing": Black box gaslighting and the power to independently know and credibly critique algorithms. *Information, Communication & Society*, *26*(6), 1226–1243.

Gong, Y., Shang, L., & Wang, D. (2024). Integrating social explanations into explainable artificial intelligence (XAI) for combating misinformation: Vision and challenges. *IEEE Transactions on Computational Social Systems*, *11*(5), 6705–6726.

Gull, U., Iqbal, A., & Idrees, U. (2023). Lack of communication ethics and social responsibility over social media. *Online Media and Society*, *4*(4), 15–31.

Hanlon, A., & Jones, K. (2023). Ethical concerns about social media privacy policies: Do users have the ability to understand their consent actions?. *Journal of Strategic Marketing*, 1–18.

Herden, C. J., Alliu, E., Cakici, A., Cormier, T., Deguelle, C., Gambhir, S., Griffiths, C., Gupta, S., Kamani, S. R., Kiratli, Y.-S., Kispataki, M., Lange, G., Matos, L. M. de, Moreno, L. T., Nunez, H. A. B., Pilla, V., Raj, B., Roe, J., Skoda, M., . . . & Edinger-Schons, L. M. (2021). "Corporate digital responsibility" New corporate responsibilities in the digital age. In *Sustainability management forum| NachhaltigkeitsManagementForum* (Vol. 29, No. 1, pp. 13–29). Springer Berlin Heidelberg.

Hong, J. S., Longoni, C., & Morwitz, V. G. (2024). Proximity bias: Interactive effect of spatial distance and outcome valence on probability judgments. *Journal of Consumer Psychology*, *34*(1), 18–34.

Just, N., & Saurwein, F. (2024). Enhancing social-media regulation through transparency? Examining the new transparency regime in the EU. *TechREG Chronicle*, *2024*(2), online.

Kollnig, K., Shuba, A., Van Kleek, M., Binns, R., & Shadbolt, N. (2022). Goodbye tracking? Impact of iOS app tracking transparency and privacy labels. In *Proceedings of the 2022 ACM conference on fairness, accountability, and transparency* (pp. 508–520). Association for Computing Machinery.

Lipschultz, J. H. (2023). *Social media communication: Concepts, practices, data, law and ethics*. Routledge.

Lybeck, R., Koiranen, I., & Koivula, A. (2024). From digital divide to digital capital: The role of education and digital skills in social media participation. *Universal Access in the Information Society*, *23*(4), 1657–1669.

Malkin, N. (2022). Contextual integrity, explained: A more usable privacy definition. *IEEE Security & Privacy*, *21*(1), 58–65.

Mazhar, K., & Dwivedi, P. (2024). Decoding the black box: LIME-assisted understanding of convolutional neural network (CNN) in classification of social media tweets. *Social Network Analysis and Mining*, *14*(1), 133.

Montag, C., & Elhai, J. D. (2023). On social media design, (online-) time well-spent and addictive behaviors in the age of surveillance capitalism. *Current Addiction Reports*, *10*(3), 610–616.

Reiberg, A. (2022). Transparency and surveillance of end users on social media platforms. *Trust and Transparency in an Age of Surveillance*, *165*.

Saniuk, S., & Grabowska, S. (2022). *Development of knowledge and skills of engineers and managers in the era of Industry 5.0 in the light of expert research*. Notebooks Scientific. Organization and Management/Silesian University of Technology.

Saurwein, F., & Spencer-Smith, C. (2021). Automated trouble: The role of algorithmic selection in harms on social media platforms. *Media and Communication*, *9*(4), 222–233.

Shahidzadeh, M. H., & Shokouhyar, S. (2024). Unveiling just-in-time decision support system using social media analytics: A case study on reverse logistics resource recycling. *Industrial Management & Data Systems, 124*(6), 2251–2283.

Sharma, M., Huertas, L., Shah, S., Gil, A., Bitrian, E., & Chang, T. C. (2024). Compliance with web content accessibility guidelines in ophthalmology social media posts. *Scientific Reports, 14*(1), 9142.

Yang, Z., & Ge, Z. (2022). On paradigm of industrial big data analytics: From evolution to revolution. *IEEE Transactions on Industrial Informatics, 18*(12), 8373–8388.

Zhang, H., Zang, Z., Zhu, H., Uddin, M. I., & Amin, M. A. (2022). Big data-assisted social media analytics for business model for business decision making system competitive analysis. *Information Processing & Management, 59*(1), 102762.

Zhou, X., He, C., Chen, X., & Zhang, Y. (2024). HSAP: A human-in-the-loop social media-based situation awareness platform. *Proceedings of the VLDB Endowment, 17*(12), 4493–4496.

6 Strategies, tools, and competencies in the face of digital transformation

Integration of strategic, technological, and ethical perspectives in management

Contemporary strategic management, confronted with the dynamics of digital transformation, must transcend traditional planning frameworks. It is no longer sufficient to treat technology solely as a tool for cost optimization or operational support. The key to achieving sustainable competitive advantage and business legitimacy lies in integrating strategic, technological, and ethical perspectives at the highest level of corporate planning. This process provides an indispensable foundation for formulating a digital strategy that is both effective and responsible.

Central to this integration is ensuring strategic alignment of technologies (strategic alignment). We must move away from implementing technology for its own sake and focus on the conscious use of digital tools such as AI, the IoT, and Big Data to create new business value. A digital strategy must clearly define how adopting a given technology will impact the business model—whether it will enable entry into new markets and redefine the customer value proposition—and how it will impact our competitive advantage. This requires management not only to have a thorough understanding of technological potential but also the ability to translate it into measurable strategic outcomes, seamlessly integrating the technological perspective with business objectives (Wang et al., 2021).

However, the strategic use of advanced technologies, especially those based on data and algorithms, poses a number of significant ethical challenges. Therefore, it is essential that, in parallel with technological investment planning, an ethical framework be incorporated into the strategy. This means that a digital strategy must incorporate mechanisms for responsible technology management, essential for maintaining stakeholder trust and ensuring a social license to innovate. Key ethical considerations that should be embedded in the strategic process include ensuring transparency and explainability of decision-making systems and actively managing the risk of bias and prejudice (bias mitigation), which may be unconsciously implemented by algorithms. Incorporating

DOI: 10.4324/9781003730507-7

these principles at the strategic level minimizes legal and reputational risks and allows ethics to be treated not as a regulatory burden but as a source of strategic differentiation and advantage (Venugopal et al., 2024).

Ultimately, even the best-designed digital strategy, technologically and ethically integrated, will remain a dead letter without adequate change management and shaping of organizational culture. Digital transformation is, in fact, largely a human transformation. Therefore, the strategy must actively support mechanisms for developing competencies and attitudes necessary to support dynamic technological development while maintaining established ethical standards. This means promoting flexibility and a culture of continuous learning, as well as enforcing interdisciplinary responsibility, in which specialists in technology, business strategy, and ethics collaborate from the earliest stages of innovation design. It is here, in the context of human capital and organizational culture, that a digital strategy ultimately integrates all three perspectives, ensuring the long-term resilience and legitimacy of the organization in a dynamically changing digital environment (Nørgård, 2021).

The integration of strategic, technological, and ethical perspectives is most evident in efforts that deliberately balance innovation with responsibility, moving from abstract vision to operational accountability. Consider the voice assistant initiatives pursued by tech giants. From a strategic perspective, these companies aim to expand the digital services ecosystem and establish a new, voice-based customer interface, which in turn increases customer retention and data monetization potential. From a technological perspective, this requires the implementation of advanced NLP and ML systems, which entails managing a massive, sensitive cloud infrastructure. This is where strategic and technological ambitions collide with ethical perspectives, placing privacy at the center. The success of this strategy depends on implementing rigorous opt-out, anonymization, and data encryption mechanisms. The need to transparently communicate how voice recordings are stored and used is not only a regulatory requirement but also a strategic safeguard, as the loss of user trust could undermine the entire strategy adopted (Wixom et al., 2023).

Shifting our attention to the manufacturing sector, strategic integration is evident in investments in three-dimensional (3D) printing (additive manufacturing). From a strategic perspective, this technology facilitates large-scale product personalization, shortens lead times, and increases supply chain flexibility, which is crucial for responding rapidly to market demands. Technologically, this requires the integration of digital systems [computer-aided design/computer-aided manufacturing (CAD/CAM)] with operational systems within the Industry 4.0 paradigm. Crucially, the inclusion of ethical and environmental perspectives is essential. This strategy directly supports sustainable development goals, as additive manufacturing generates less material waste, and local, on-demand production reduces the carbon footprint associated with transportation. In this case, technological innovation becomes a tool for implementing CSR (Saniuk et al., 2023).

Continuing our discussion of integrating perspectives in management, after discussing the strategic framework, it becomes crucial to deepen the analysis at the operational and technological levels. While the digital strategy defines the direction and goals, the actual shape of the transformation is determined by the specific tools and technologies the organization implements. It is in their daily use—from Big-data analysis to the implementation of AI—that the most pressing ethical dilemmas arise, requiring accountability to be embedded directly into the systems' architecture.

Data and privacy management are paramount. The implementation of advanced analytical systems and cloud platforms, while strategically essential for data-driven decision-making, poses significant challenges in data governance. Technological tools must not only effectively collect, process, and analyze data but also ensure its security and privacy. Ethical integration requires that these platforms be designed in accordance with the privacy by design principle, where encryption, anonymization, pseudonymization, and access control mechanisms are built into the system from the outset, not added as an afterthought. This is not only a requirement for compliance with regulations such as the GDPR but also a condition for maintaining customer trust and strategic legitimacy (Ruggiu et al., 2022).

Continuing, the most complex ethical challenges arise in the context of AI-based decision-making systems. AI, as a technological tool with a profound impact on business processes and customer lives (e.g., in recruitment, credit assessment, and marketing profiling), requires specialized ethical tools. The issue of bias and prejudice becomes crucial here. The historical data on which algorithms are trained often reflects social discrimination. Technological tools must be equipped with mechanisms to actively detect and mitigate bias, which requires continuous monitoring of fairness metrics and the intervention of data engineers and analysts. Furthermore, ethics require transparency, leading to the need to implement XAI tools. These tools provide the ability to explain how an algorithm reached a given decision, which is essential both for internal auditability and for fulfilling the customer's right to receive clear justification in the event of a negative decision.

Finally, tools and technologies must support systemic accountability. In the context of digital transformation, where decisions are often autonomous, implementing auditability and accountability systems is essential. This means designing mechanisms that record every human and automated intervention, as well as establishing clear human-in-the-loop procedures, defining the moments at which the autonomous process must be interrupted and submitted for human review. Such a technological oversight framework becomes a bridge between innovation and ethical integrity, ensuring that the adopted tools not only increase efficiency but also strengthen trust and minimize systemic risk (Huleihel & Refael, 2024).

Moving on to the final and most anthropocentric element of integration, this segment focuses on competencies and organizational culture. This is key to closing the triad, as even the best-defined strategy and the most advanced tools will remain ineffective without the appropriate capabilities and ethos within the organization. Moving from the level of planning (strategy) and tools (technology) to practical implementation, we realize that digital transformation is, above all, a cultural transformation. Therefore, an effective digital strategy must conclude with an action plan that not only defines new competencies but also actively builds a culture based on accountability, transparency, and innovation. This means strategically empowering the human factor as the primary catalyst for ethical innovation.

In this context, defining hybrid competencies that combine technical knowledge with strategic thinking and ethical awareness becomes a fundamental challenge. Equipping digital leaders with the ability to understand technologies (e.g., AI fundamentals) as sources of strategic value, not just operational costs, is crucial. At the same time, leaders are required to champion ethical values, able to lead complex discussions about the risks associated with algorithms and data protection. Simultaneously, the strategy must anticipate comprehensive employee development and retraining. In addition to purely technical skills such as data analytics, soft skills are equally crucial. These include critical evaluation of algorithmic decisions, flexibility, and interdisciplinary collaboration, particularly between engineers, lawyers, and managers. In this way, investing in people becomes a direct component of achieving strategic goals.

However, strengthening competencies must be supported by an appropriate organizational culture. This culture acts as a feedback mechanism, enabling the achievement of strategic goals while adhering to ethical frameworks. In practice, this means that the organization must view ethics and sustainability as an integral part of innovation, not as a brake. It is essential to create an environment in which employees feel obligated and safe to raise ethical red flags (whistleblowing) regarding the design of AI tools or data collection. Furthermore, because technology is evolving rapidly, the strategy must foster a culture of experimentation and continuous learning, ready to immediately correct course when new ethical or regulatory challenges arise. Only under such conditions can change management become an ongoing process, not a one-time initiative.

In summary, competencies and organizational culture constitute the ultimate bridge between an ambitious strategic vision and technological complexity with the requirement of ethical responsibility. Investing in people and their work ethic guarantees that digital transformation will be not only effective and innovative but also sustainable and trustworthy in the long term, ultimately completing the strategic-technological-ethical triad.

While strategy provides direction and technology provides the tools, competencies and organizational culture constitute the ultimate culmination of the responsible transformation triad. In practice, this means that leaders must intentionally invest in HR development to transform abstract ethical frameworks into operational actions.

In this context, a key step is developing hybrid talent, capable of seamlessly combining technical expertise with strategic thinking and ethical awareness. McKinsey & Company exemplifies this approach by strategically investing in staff development within McKinsey Digital. Consultants are trained not only in advanced analytics and AI implementations but also in the identification and mitigation of algorithmic bias and in ensuring AI (XAI) explainability for clients. Therefore, the ability to lead discussions on regulatory and reputational risks associated with technology is becoming a key strategic competency, offered to clients as a value proposition, not just a legal requirement.

Moreover, effective ethics implementation requires formal governance mechanisms that embed accountability into processes. Microsoft embraces this principle by establishing formal, cross-functional oversight bodies, such as the Office of Responsible AI (ORA) and the AI, Ethics, and Effects in Engineering and Research (Aether) Committee. These bodies play a key role in embedding ethical frameworks directly into product design. Teams composed of engineers, researchers, and policy experts assess the social and ethical implications of new AI products before they reach market. Adopting this culture of "ethics by design" makes systemic accountability an integral part of technology roadmaps.

Ultimately, for these competencies and mechanisms to function effectively, a supportive culture of flexibility and accountability is essential. Netflix, for example, promotes a culture based on high autonomy and constant experimentation, enabling rapid adaptation to technological and market changes. Although teams have considerable freedom to test new technological solutions, this autonomy is closely linked to direct accountability for results, including recommendation algorithms and their impact on user behavior. Employees are encouraged to think critically and analyze, allowing for the rapid identification and course correction of ethical or social issues. Such a learning culture is essential for maintaining a strategic advantage, ensuring that innovations are implemented effectively and ethically, thus encapsulating the strategic-technological-ethical triad.

Systemic management of digital and reputational risk

Effective digital transformation requires recognizing that every technological innovation carries commensurate systemic risk that transcends traditional IT governance. A strategic shift away from siloed risk management (e.g., separate for cybersecurity, operations, and legal) toward an integrated risk management (IRM) approach is essential. This new strategy aims to view risk as a value-based management element, not just a cost, integrating operational, technological, and strategic risk assessment processes into a single, coherent decision-making platform. Furthermore, in an era of complex ecosystems, extending this control to the external ecosystem is crucial. Strategies must address third-party risks stemming from the digital supply chain and dependencies on cloud providers, which create complex legal, operational, and security risks (Liew, 2022).

To address these challenges, organizations must invest in advanced digital risk assessment tools and methods. In cloud environments, where security configurations are dynamic, continuous cloud security posture management (CSPM) tools are essential, which automatically monitor configurations and detect vulnerabilities in real time. Quantitative methods, leveraging predictive analytics and Big Data, are also used to forecast security incidents and estimate potential financial losses. This shifts risk management from reactive to proactive. Attack simulations and penetration testing (e.g., Red Team/Blue Team methods), which continuously test systems' resilience to breach attempts, also remain critical technological controls (Xia et al., 2021).

The issues discussed earlier lead directly to reputational risk management, which, in the digital age, often arises from technological failures. This risk requires proactive strategies and specialized tools, such as advanced social media monitoring. These systems allow for the rapid identification and neutralization of negative trends, disinformation, or online crises before they escalate into full-blown brand threats. At the same time, organizations must develop contingency plans for the risk of "algorithmic error"—a situation in which AI systems generate harmful or unethical results. This means being prepared for open and transparent crisis communication following a data breach, focusing on quickly, honestly, and responsibly informing stakeholders to rebuild trust, a key competency in crisis management (Srinivas & Liang, 2022).

Ultimately, effective risk control depends on competencies and governance at all levels. Continuously minimizing human risk (the most common attack vector) through cyber hygiene and employee awareness programs is essential. At the same time, ensuring board oversight is essential to ensure that digital and reputational risks are regularly and clearly reported at the highest level. This approach, in which education and governance structures are aligned with technology and strategy, is the only way to systematically manage the complexity of digital risk in a transforming organization (Wong & Floridi, 2023).

Continuing the analysis of systemic digital risk management, it is now time to focus on practical tools and methods that enable organizations to effectively assess, monitor, and control threats in a dynamic transformation environment. In this segment, we expand on the topic "Digital risk assessment tools and methods". The effectiveness of a digital risk management strategy depends directly on the accuracy and proactivity of the tools used. In an era when infrastructure is moving to distributed and cloud-based environments, implementing mechanisms for continuous monitoring and automated security validation becomes crucial. In this context, continuous CSPM tools are essential. Their role is to audit security configurations in real time across all cloud services [Infrastructure as a Service (IaaS), Platform as a Service (PaaS), and Software as a Service (SaaS)], automatically identifying misconfigurations and noncompliance with internal policies and regulatory standards. This shift from sporadic verification to continuous oversight is the foundation of modern technological control, minimizing risks arising from dynamic infrastructure changes (Jim, 2024).

However, technological control must be complemented by advanced quantitative risk analysis methods. To this end, organizations are increasingly leveraging Big Data and predictive analytics. This approach allows them to go beyond traditional, qualitative risk assessments, enabling them to predict security incidents and estimate the potential financial loss resulting from a system failure or cyberattack. These tools analyze historical data on incidents, user behavior patterns, and vulnerabilities, generating risk metrics that are directly linked to business value. As a result, risk management becomes a data-driven process, enabling strategic allocation of security resources where risk (and potential loss) is highest.

Finally, technological control tools must be validated through practical resilience testing. Methodologies such as Attack Simulation and Penetration Testing—often conducted by Red Teams (attackers) and Blue Teams (defenders)—are an essential element of validation. These tests simulate realistic threat scenarios, taking into account both advanced hacking methods and vulnerabilities resulting from human error. This provides an organization with a clear picture of its actual resilience to cyber threats and allows it to systematically strengthen its defenses. Integrating these technical tools, from cloud monitoring and predictive analytics to attack simulations, enables systemic risk management, transforming the security department from a cost center into a strategic business partner (Damaraju, 2022).

Adopting effective digital risk management methods leads directly to challenges related to reputational risk—the most ephemeral and simultaneously most costly consequence of technological failures. In this segment, we expand on the topic "Reputational risk management in the digital environment". In the digital age, where information spreads globally and instantaneously, reputational risk is no longer simply a consequence of strategic errors but often a direct consequence of technological failures or ethical algorithmic errors. Therefore, managing this risk requires proactive strategies and specialized digital tools. A key strategy is continuous monitoring and rapid response to digital crises. This includes implementing advanced social media monitoring and sentiment analysis tools, which enable the rapid identification of negative trends, disinformation, or hate attacks on online platforms. Speed of response is critical, allowing for neutralization of the threat before it escalates into a full-blown, systemic reputational crisis.

Moreover, these risks are closely linked to an organization's internal systems, necessitating the systematic management of algorithmic failure risk. Companies must develop detailed contingency and communication plans in the event that autonomous AI systems produce unethical, discriminatory, or harmful outcomes (e.g., a customer error that goes viral). Such an event directly undermines public trust, requiring communication procedures to ensure accountability for algorithmic actions (Min & Borch, 2022).

Finally, a key element of this strategy is transparency and crisis communication, which aims to rebuild trust. In the event of incidents such as data breaches, organizations must have developed competencies in open and honest communication. Rather than downplaying the problem's magnitude, the emphasis is on informing stakeholders quickly, fully, and responsibly about the scope, causes, and remedial measures of the incident. Only such an approach, treating communication as a strategic risk management function rather than simply a PR response, will allow for regaining the social license to innovate and maintaining reputations in the long term.

Continuing our systematic discussion of risk management in digital transformation, we turn to the topic of risk management competencies and governance. This final segment concludes the analysis by focusing on the human and structural mechanisms that transform strategy and tools into effective action. Even the most advanced digital risk assessment tools and the most well-formulated reputation strategies will not be effective without appropriate governance structures and human competencies. Systemic risk is largely a human risk, resulting from operational errors, lack of awareness, or inadequate oversight.

Therefore, a key element of proactive risk management is minimizing human risk through educational programs. It is essential to implement cyber hygiene and employee awareness programs that go beyond traditional training and focus on building a culture of security. These programs must be ongoing and engaging, aimed at minimizing the most common attack vectors—phishing, social engineering, and system misconfigurations. Employees, as the first line of defense, must be equipped with the necessary competencies to identify and respond to threats. This is a fundamental strategy for cultural transformation in risk control.

Equally important is a strategic approach to risk at the highest decision-making level, as implemented by board oversight. In the context of digital transformation, risk must be regularly, clearly, and comprehensively reported to the management and supervisory board levels. The goal is not only to meet compliance requirements but, above all, to enable strategic investment decisions in security and control mechanisms. The board must treat digital risk as a business risk, not just a technical one. This requires appropriate digital competencies among board members to effectively oversee and challenge risk management policies (Wong & Floridi, 2023).

Ultimately, effective digital and reputational risk management requires adopting a zero trust architecture at the governance level. This strategy, while technological, is primarily a management philosophy that assumes that no user, device, or application, whether inside or outside the network, is trustworthy by default. This translates into rigorous access verification mechanisms and constant monitoring, crucial in the dynamic and distributed environment of digital transformation. Such an integrated approach—combining employee awareness, board oversight, and a rigorous governance framework—is essential for systemic risk management and business continuity (He et al., 2022).

From a governance perspective, the introduction of independent audit and control mechanisms adapted to the speed of digital change is crucial. Traditional annual audits are no longer sufficient. Organizations must strategically implement continuous auditing and continuous monitoring systems that leverage advanced data analytics to continuously verify transactions, processes, and security configurations. Such proactive oversight aims not only to detect but also to immediately correct system or process deficiencies before they escalate into a serious incident. This represents an evolution from static, periodic verification to a dynamic, integrated internal control system that operates at the pace of digital transformation, thus fostering a culture of zero tolerance for irregularities.

Next, in the context of governance, it is necessary to establish an interdisciplinary Digital Risk and Ethics Committee at the executive level. This committee should bring together representatives from IT, security, legal, HR, and strategic business management. Its primary role is to transcend organizational silos, ensure that technological decisions take into account reputational and ethical risks, and harmonize internal security policies with external regulations (e.g., AI Act and GDPR). This structure acts as a strategic filtering mechanism, assessing innovation projects not only for ROI but also for potential systemic and societal risks, ensuring that governance is integrated across all dimensions of the transformation (Caner & Evgin, 2021).

Finally, future-proof risk management requires the strategic integration of external verification and benchmarking. Companies cannot rely solely on their own audit mechanisms; they must actively engage external experts in cybersecurity and AI ethics to conduct independent resilience tests and ethical audits of algorithms. This external validation provides an objective assessment of risk management maturity and identifies hidden gaps in adopted strategies and tools. By constantly benchmarking their standards against market best practices and evolving ethical norms, organizations not only build stronger security measures but also strengthen their credibility and reputation in the eyes of regulators and key stakeholders.

The theoretical analysis presented earlier is supported by corporate practice, where systematic digital and reputational risk management is crucial to the survival and success of businesses in the digital age. The examples presented later illustrate how key organizations are integrating strategies, tools, and competencies to proactively manage these complex risks.

In the financial sector, where cyber and regulatory threats are at their highest, the strategy is to implement IRM, supported by AI. Many global financial institutions have experienced significant financial and reputational losses due to fraud, which traditional methods detected too slowly. The use of AI-based predictive analytics (as in the example of a bank that implemented advanced models) allows for the identification of patterns of irregular activity in real time across large sets of transactions and customer behavior. Technologically, these systems are integrated with existing infrastructure (so-called *seamless integration*), enabling real-time analysis and reducing fraud response times by 45% or more. This shift from reaction to anticipation is the essence of systemic risk management and leads to significant increases in operational efficiency.

In response to tightening regulations in Europe, such as the Digital Operational Resilience Act (DORA), companies in critical sectors are strategically investing in tools that ensure continuous monitoring of information and communication technology (ICT) systems and operational compliance. This is a direct example of how regulatory strategy translates into the need for specific tools. Endpoint management platforms (Endpoint Central) and privileged access management (PAM360) are being implemented to not only monitor the security status of endpoint devices but also to automatically deploy updates and test business continuity plans through disaster simulation. Digital and operational risks are managed through continuous readiness verification, and compliance reporting against standards (e.g., ISO 27001 and DORA) is automated, increasing credibility and protecting the company's reputation from regulatory penalties.

Digital risk is systemic, as the example of a large European aluminum producer that fell victim to a sophisticated cyberattack perfectly illustrates. This attack not only paralyzed the manufacturer's operations but also had a global impact, disrupting supply chains and distribution for business partners in multiple countries. Although this incident was by definition a cyber risk, it triggered an immediate web of interconnected risks: business interruption, loss of consumer trust, devaluation of shares, and widespread reputational damage. This case highlights the need for IRM to encompass the entire ecosystem, and third-party risk management strategies are crucial. The success of digital risk management is therefore measured by the ability to protect not only one's own network but also the business continuity of its partners.

At the governance and competency levels, global organizations are strategically adopting recognized cybersecurity frameworks—such as the National Institute of Standards and Technology (NIST) Cybersecurity Framework (especially for critical infrastructure) or International Organization for Standardization (ISO) 27001 (for a global Information Security Management System). These frameworks serve not only as a checklist but also as a systematic risk management tool. By implementing ISO 27001, companies formally establish continuous monitoring and regular audits, and assign responsibility for risk management to senior leaders. This formal process of occupational risk assessment and risk treatment (through transfer, reduction, or acceptance) raises the level of digital competency within management and ensures transparency in communicating risk tolerance throughout the organization.

Building a culture of responsibility and continuous learning

A culture of accountability and continuous learning is an essential pillar for an organization pursuing digital transformation. It constitutes a value system that allows for flexible adaptation to rapidly changing technologies while maintaining ethical integrity. Therefore, the strategy must actively support an agile and experimentation mindset, which strategically views errors not as a reason for punishment but as data for optimization. Implementing a "fail fast, learn faster" approach requires establishing safe environments for experimentation (technology sandboxes) where teams can confidently test new digital solutions. This cultural mindset must be supported by a continuous improvement strategy (digital Kaizen), implementing systems that automate the collection of feedback (feedback loop) from implemented digital solutions. Such mechanisms ensure that innovations are continuously refined and optimized based on empirical data, minimizing the risk of errors being perpetuated (Lizarelli et al., 2025).

Further cultivating this mindset requires leveraging modern tools and platforms to support knowledge and collaboration. Digital transformation is inherently dynamic, so training programs must evolve. Implementing learning on demand (LOD) and micro-learning is essential to delivering personalized, contextual knowledge precisely when employees need it (Just-in-Time Learning). At the same time, breaking down silos through cross-departmental collaboration tools is key to integrated learning. Leveraging digital platforms to create cross-functional teams that combine technological, business, and ethical expertise is becoming a strategic imperative. This not only enables effective complex problem-solving but also accelerates horizontal knowledge transfer.

Furthermore, to embed accountability, it is necessary to establish formal governance and competencies that support this ethos. This is achieved by implementing clear algorithmic accountability models, such as detailed accountability matrices [responsible, accountable, consulted and informed (RACI)], which precisely define who is responsible for the outcomes and consequences of decisions made by autonomous systems. Accountability must be assigned in a transparent and auditable manner. For this purpose, formal roles are increasingly being established, such as the chief ethics officer (CEO), whose primary responsibility is to serve as a cultural catalyst, fostering dialogue on organizational values and integrating ethical perspectives into all new projects. This is complemented by a learning reward and accountability system, where incentive systems recognize not only the achievement of business goals but also active participation in skill development, reporting potential ethical issues, and proactive knowledge sharing. This integrated approach—spanning culture, tools, and structures—is a prerequisite for a transformation in which innovation is closely aligned with trust.

A culture of accountability and continuous learning must be strategically embedded in daily operational practices, extending beyond formal training. A key tool supporting this shift is the implementation of retrospective methods and post-mortems for digital projects. This practice, a systematic and blameless analysis of technological and ethical failures, focuses on identifying the systemic causes of errors rather than individual fault. As a result, teams document lessons learned, which are then standardized and distributed throughout the organization, enriching the corporate knowledge base. This enables rapid course correction and minimizes the risk of repeating mistakes, effectively transforming failures into intellectual capital.

For learning to be truly "continuous" and "systemic", a strategic approach to knowledge architecture and digital inclusion is essential. This architecture involves the creation of central, easily accessible knowledge repositories, such as advanced KMSs, which function as interactive platforms facilitating expert knowledge exchange. Strategically, DI becomes an ethical requirement, ensuring that all employees—regardless of prior competencies—have equitable access to learning resources and are fully integrated into the transformation process. This is crucial because systemic responsibility for technology must be shared by everyone, not just IT specialists, fundamentally strengthening a company's cultural resilience to change and new ethical challenges (Pekkala, 2024).

Furthermore, future-proof management requires the implementation of independent audit and control mechanisms that adapt to the pace of change. Traditional annual audits are insufficient. Hence, the strategic need to implement continuous auditing and continuous monitoring systems that leverage analytics to constantly verify transactions, processes, and security configurations. This evolution toward a dynamic, integrated internal control system operates at the pace of digital transformation, fostering a culture of zero tolerance for irregularities. This approach not only protects the system but also establishes operational transparency, which is the foundation of cultural accountability.

The final step in ensuring systemic accountability is the establishment of an interdisciplinary Digital Risk and Ethics Committee at the executive level. This committee, composed of experts from various fields (IT, law, and HR), serves as a strategic filtering mechanism that evaluates innovative projects not only for ROI but also for potential systemic and societal risks. Its operation harmonizes internal security policies with external regulations and ensures that governance is integrated across all dimensions of the transformation. This is where all the perspectives discussed—strategic, technological, and ethical—come together into a cohesive, vibrant culture capable of continuous self-improvement and responsible action (Caner & Evgin, 2021).

Effectively building a culture of continuous learning requires moving away from traditional, centralized training models toward dynamic, integrated platforms that provide the technological infrastructure for flexibility and accountability. In this context, implementing systems that enable employees to access knowledge precisely when they need it (just-in-time learning) is a strategic imperative. This is achieved through the use of learning experience platforms (LXPs) and micro-learning solutions. These tools deliver personalized, short learning modules (e.g., simulations and contextual instruction) embedded directly in the work context. This approach not only significantly increases engagement and knowledge retention but also allows employees to quickly acquire new skills related to specific digital projects, thereby enhancing the organization's competency agility (Nilmanee et al., 2024).

However, a culture of accountability and learning is inherently linked to effective cross-functional collaboration, which digital technologies must strategically support. Tools must serve as catalysts that break down traditional organizational silos. Leveraging advanced digital workplace platforms—which integrate communication, project management, and knowledge-sharing systems—enables the creation and support of cross-functional teams. These platforms become the technological foundation for expert knowledge management, facilitating horizontal knowledge exchange between technology, business, and ethics departments. Such exchange is absolutely crucial for IRM and the responsible design of digital solutions.

Furthermore, organizations are strategically leveraging gamification and simulations to increase engagement and achieve lasting behavioral change. This is particularly effective for cybersecurity and ethics training, where human error poses the greatest risk. These tools, for example, through realistic phishing simulations or interactive scenarios involving AI ethical dilemmas, allow employees to practically practice responsibility and make complex, moral decisions in a safe environment. By transforming theoretical knowledge into instinctive, responsible behavior, gamification and simulations are crucial for minimizing human risk and strengthening ethical conduct within organizations.

For learning and collaboration platforms to become a part of systemic management, they must be directly incorporated into operational processes (embedding knowledge into workflows). It's not enough for employees to possess knowledge; they must have access to it at the point of use. This is achieved by integrating KMS with project management tools (e.g., Jira and Asana) and risk and compliance management [governance, risk and compliance (GRC)] systems. If an engineer designs a new algorithm, the system automatically displays contextual ethical guidelines and links to retrospectives from previous projects (lessons learned) relevant to the given stage of work. This solution ensures that operational accountability is supported by real-time knowledge, thereby improving decision quality and minimizing the risk of errors arising from cognitive bias.

A culture of continuous learning is strongest when driven by internal experts, not just formal HR departments. Establishing a formal digital mentoring and change ambassador network is strategic here. These are internal experts (e.g., engineers with high ethical awareness and analysts with strong communication skills) who act as catalysts and internal coaches on a peer-to-peer basis. Their role is to transfer advanced technological knowledge and foster a culture of accountability within front-line operational teams, ensuring that new competencies are not only learned but also applied and replicated throughout the organization. This decentralized learning model fosters a sense of shared responsibility for digital transformation (Whitson, 2021).

Effectively building a culture of accountability cannot be merely a set of ethical recommendations; it must be embedded in a formal governance structure and supported by precisely defined roles and competencies. A key element of governance is the implementation of clear algorithmic accountability models. This is achieved by establishing precise accountability matrices (RACIs) that define in detail who is responsible for the outcomes, validation, and consequences of decisions made by autonomous systems. Accountability must be assigned in an auditable and transparent manner, extending beyond the technology itself—including data owners, modelers, and those approving the implementation. This formalization ensures that the ethical aspects of the technology are treated as strategic risks, not just operational ones.

Supporting this rigorous governance requires establishing key roles and competencies, including the appointment of an ethics officer or a CEO, who acts as both a cultural catalyst and a strategic facilitator. This individual's competencies must combine legal and ethical expertise with an understanding of technology and business objectives. This individual's role is to manage the value dialogue, promote transparency, and actively incorporate ethical perspectives into each new digital project, acting as an internal cultural auditor and advisor to the board. This role ensures that the ethical framework is continually updated to address rapidly evolving technological challenges (Yue et al., 2023).

References

Caner, N., & Evgin, D. (2021). Digital risks and adolescents: The relationships between digital game addiction, emotional eating, and aggression. *International Journal of Mental Health Nursing*, *30*(6), 1599–1609.

Damaraju, A. (2022). Social media cybersecurity: Protecting personal and business information. *International Journal of Advanced Engineering Technologies and Innovations*, *1*(2), 50–69.

He, Y., Huang, D., Chen, L., Ni, Y., & Ma, X. (2022). A survey on zero trust architecture: Challenges and future trends. *Wireless Communications and Mobile Computing*, *2022*(1), 6476274.

Huleihel, W., & Refael, Y. (2024). Mathematical framework for online social media auditing. *Journal of Machine Learning Research*, *25*(64), 1–40.

Jim, M. M. I. (2024). Cloud security posture management automating risk identification and response in cloud infrastructures. *Academic Journal on Science, Technology, Engineering & Mathematics Education*, *4*(3), 10–69593.

Liew, C. L. (2022). Let's talk about risks: A pillar framework for social media risk management in memory institutions. *Online Information Reviews*, *46*(2), 375–390.

Lizarelli, F. L., Antony, J., Suarez, M., Carneiro, F., Sony, M., Chakraborty, A., Ma, J., & Chan, F. T. (2025). Analysis of the impact of Kaizen practices on ESG performance and the mediating role of digital systems. *Business Process Management Journal*, *31*(8), 148–175.

Min, B. H., & Borch, C. (2022). Systemic failures and organizational risk management in algorithmic trading: Normal accidents and high reliability in financial markets. *Social Studies of Science*, *52*(2), 277–302.

Nilmanee, T., Sintanakul, K., & Sakulviriyakitkul, P. (2024). The design of a learning experience platform using xapi with design thinking learning to promote innovation. *International Journal of Emerging Technologies in Learning (IJET)*, *19*(1), 54–67.

Nørgård, R. T. (2021). Theorizing hybrid lifelong learning. *British Journal of Educational Technology*, *52*(4), 1709–1723.

Pekkala, K. (2024). Digital inclusion and inequalities at work in the age of social media. *Human Resource Management Journal*, *34*(3), 540–559.

Ruggiu, D., Blok, V., Coenen, C., Kalloniatis, C., Kitsiou, A., Mavroeidi, A. G., Milani, S., & Sitzia, A. (2022). Responsible innovation at work: Gamification, public engagement, and privacy by design. *Journal of Responsible Innovation*, *9*(3), 315–343.

Saniuk, S., Grabowska, S., & Fahlevi, M. (2023). Personalization of products and sustainable production and consumption in the context of industry 5.0. In *Industry 5.0: Creative and innovative organizations* (pp. 55–70). Springer International Publishing.

Srinivas, S., & Liang, H. (2022). Being digital to being vulnerable: Does digital transformation allure a data breach?. *Journal of Electronic Business & Digital Economics*, *1*(1/2), 111–137.

Venugopal, J. P., Subramanian, A. A. V., Sundaram, G., Rivera, M., & Wheeler, P. (2024). A comprehensive approach to bias mitigation for sentiment analysis of social media data. *Applied Sciences*, *14*(23), 11471.

Wang, Y., Deng, Q., Rod, M., & Ji, S. (2021). A thematic exploration of social media analytics in marketing research and an agenda for future inquiry. *Journal of Strategic Marketing*, *29*(6), 471–491.

Whitson, B. A. (2021). Mentorship, sponsorship, and the emerging role of social media. *The Annals of Thoracic Surgery*, *114*(2), 598.

Wixom, B. H., Beath, C. M., & Owens, L. (2023). *Data is everybody's business: The fundamentals of data monetization*. Myth Press.

Wong, D., & Floridi, L. (2023). Meta's oversight board: A review and critical assessment. *Minds and Machines*, *33*(2), 261–284.

Xia, T., Washizaki, H., Fukazawa, Y., Kaiya, H., Ogata, S., Fernandez, E. B., Kato, T., Kanuka, H., Okubo, T., Yoshioka, N., & Hazeyama, A. (2021). CSPM: Metamodel for handling security and privacy knowledge in cloud service development. *International Journal of Systems and Software Security and Protection (IJSSSP)*, *12*(2), 68–85.

Yue, C. A., Men, L. R., & Hart, E. B. (2023). "Chief engagement officers?" A comparative study between US corporate and nonprofit executive leaders' social media communication strategies. *Nonprofit Management and Leadership*, *33*(4), 879–892.

7 New challenges: AI, barriers to implementation, and global perspectives

The impact of AI and AI-generated content on social media management

In a context of rapid technological development, AI and AI-generated content (AIGC) have driven unprecedented changes in how businesses and organizations conduct social media management (SMM). This phenomenon goes beyond simple operational improvements; it fundamentally redefines communication, marketing, and customer engagement strategies. This analysis focuses on the comprehensive impact of these technologies, examining both their transformative potential for automation and personalization and identifying new, complex challenges—from ethical and legal issues to barriers to effective implementation and differing global perspectives—that are shaping the future of the digital communications landscape.

A central aspect of the AI revolution is the automation and radical increase in the efficiency of communication and creative processes. In this context, AIGC plays a key role, enabling the production of materials (text, graphic elements, and even video rough drafts) on an unprecedented scale. This allows marketing departments to reduce operating costs while maintaining a high publishing frequency. Furthermore, advanced AI algorithms have become the driving force behind personalization and precise targeting. By analyzing extensive sets of user behavioral data, these tools enable tailored messaging not only to segments but also to individual recipient preferences, directly translating into increased engagement and conversion rates. This is complemented by the use of AI for post-scheduling and optimization, in which predictive systems determine the ideal timing and type of content for publication, thereby maximizing the organic reach of content within dynamically changing platform algorithms (Ramkumar, 2025).

Moving from creative to strategic aspects, the use of AI in analysis and insights is equally crucial. ML enables effective management of so-called informational noise. Algorithms perform real-time monitoring and sentiment analysis for brands, products, or marketing campaigns, thus going beyond mere mention counting. These systems are capable of interpreting the emotional tone

DOI: 10.4324/9781003730507-8

of statements at scale, providing strategic information necessary to quickly respond to positive and negative trends. AI is indispensable in trend forecasting, as it identifies early signals of changes in consumer behavior and emerging viral topics, thereby enabling brands to proactively adapt their strategies and maintain a competitive advantage. Ultimately, AI-based tools are transforming user interaction and customer service. Modern chatbots and virtual assistants, supported by generative language models, are handling a significant portion of routine queries on social media platforms. This not only ensures 24/7 availability but also shortens response times, directly impacting positive customer experience (Falgoust et al., 2022).

Continuing the empirical analysis based on the authors' research (described in Chapter 2), with respect to the survey's closing questions, the question regarding the extent to which AI and AIGC influences SMM (Question 12), 50% of respondents see AI as a key tool of the future, while 30% of companies are already actively using it in daily operations, such as content optimization, communication personalization, and advanced moderation. This dominant group indicates the rapid adoption of AI tools to increase effectiveness and reach in social media. Large enterprises are pioneers, leveraging AI for strategic advantage. This contrasts with 20% of respondents who declared that they do not use AI or perceive its use as fraught with significant ethical or operational concerns. This group is most often characterized by smaller entities struggling with cost barriers or a lack of specialized knowledge, which threatens their ability to adapt.

Despite the undoubted benefits of integrating AI into SMM, the expansion of these technologies raises a number of new challenges and implementation barriers that require special strategic attention. One of the most significant concerns is ethics and credibility.

Automating decision-making and creative processes carries the risk of algorithmic bias. AI models trained on historical data can unwittingly replicate and reinforce existing social or market biases, leading to the generation of biased, inappropriate, and, in extreme cases, discriminatory content. Furthermore, the mass production of high-quality disinformation and deepfakes pose a significant threat to public trust in the authenticity of social media sources, forcing brands to implement rigorous verification protocols. In this context, the phenomenon of AI "hallucinations" also emerges, in which generative systems deliver seemingly credible but factually false information, necessitating that SMM teams verify information prior to publication (Medhat et al., 2025).

Closely related to ethics are legal issues and IP protection, constituting another significant barrier. The as-yet-unclear legal status of AIGC copyright raises serious doubts—it is unclear who formally owns the content created by the machine: the creator of the prompt (command), the AI tool provider, or the entity that implemented the technology. Furthermore, the use of user data for training AI models must strictly comply with privacy regulations (e.g., GDPR), which requires social media companies to constantly audit and be transparent about the collection and processing of information. Civil liability for damages resulting from AI content (e.g., defamation or IP infringement) is also a key, growing issue, forcing companies to introduce clear indemnity clauses and mechanisms in their contracts with AI providers.

In addition to ethical and legal challenges, technological and competency barriers are key obstacles. Implementing advanced AI systems, especially in larger organizations, often involves high upfront costs related to licensing, integration with existing SMM platforms, and maintaining the complex cloud infrastructure necessary to process large models. At the same time, a widening competency gap is observed: traditional social media teams urgently need to acquire new skills, especially in prompt engineering (creating effective commands), AI governance (principles of responsible AI oversight), and critical evaluation and verification of results generated by AI tools. This shifts responsibility from execution to system management. Successful AI implementation therefore depends not only on the technology itself but also on the organization's ability to responsibly manage it and establish internal standards of transparency in communication, that is, informing audiences when they are dealing with automatically generated content. These complex challenges force companies to develop a global risk management strategy, which in turn leads to the need to consider broader, global regulatory and market perspectives (Napoli & Adi, 2025).

Given the operational, ethical, and legal challenges outlined earlier, managing social media from an AI perspective requires a global and long-term strategic approach. This inevitable transformation does not occur in a regulatory vacuum but is strongly shaped by global and regional regulations. Analyzing the differences in approaches to AI regulation across continents is crucial for international strategies. An example is the European Union Artificial Intelligence Act (EU AI Act), which introduces a comprehensive, risk-based legal framework. By classifying AI systems based on potential harm (from unacceptable risk to minimal), these regulations will directly impact how multinational corporations manage content and targeting in the region, requiring greater transparency and compliance. This often contrasts with the more permissive approach in the United States, where technological development can be prioritized over formal regulation, and with the Asian model, which may place greater emphasis on state oversight of data. Adapting social media strategies to these divergent jurisdictions is therefore becoming a priority for companies running global campaigns.

It's important to emphasize that AI is fundamentally changing the job market and the competency profile of social media specialists. In the future, this role will evolve from a contractor to an AI curator and strategist. Automating routine tasks such as generating initial content or basic data analysis will free up HR, allowing them to focus on strategy, narrative creativity, building brand authenticity, and ethical oversight of machine-generated content. Human-AI collaboration, meaning effectively collaborating with AI tools to produce high-quality results while protecting against errors and biases, is becoming a key skill (Lai et al., 2022).

Ultimately, the future of SMM is determined by the evolution of the human-machine relationship and the ability to maintain the "human touch" in the age of hyperautomation. As more and more content is generated by machines, the value of authentic, emotional, and unique interactions increases. This means that brands must create advanced AI governance frameworks that not only minimize legal and ethical risks but also define where human interaction is essential in social communications—for example, crisis management or direct engagement with key opinion leaders. Success in this new era depends on a balanced combination of AI-powered efficiency and responsible, ethical, and authentic brand management.

Analysis of barriers to implementing strategic and ethical digital management

Implementing AI technology in SMM faces significant hurdles that go beyond technological and legal considerations, with primary emphasis on ethical and cultural barriers. These intangible factors pose a fundamental challenge to long-term brand reputation and organizational cohesion.

A key ethical barrier is the lack of trust in AI (trust deficit), largely stemming from the so-called "black box" perception. Management teams and, more importantly, target audiences struggle to fully understand the decision-making processes behind advanced algorithms. The limited interpretability of mechanisms underlying content personalization and automatic moderation raises concerns regarding the fairness and transparency of digital operations. When AI suggests a discriminatory message or selectively promotes content, and the reasons for this decision are unclear, it undermines the brand's credibility and its declared social responsibility. Maintaining public trust therefore becomes a barrier in itself, requiring the proactive implementation of explainable AI (XAI) mechanisms (Sahebi & Formosa, 2025).

This trust deficit deepens the problem of authenticity in digital communication. The greater the scale of automation and mass content generation (AIGC), the greater the risk of losing the "human touch". Consumers on social media value authentic, unique interactions that are often impossible for algorithmic systems to replicate. Brands that rely too aggressively on machine-generated content can be perceived as impersonal and insincere. This results in the erosion of emotional connections, a critical barrier to building loyalty and engagement, which calls into question the long-term strategic value of hyperautomation.

Moreover, the effective implementation of ethical digital management encounters significant internal cultural resistance within organizations themselves. This transformation is not only about technology but, above all, about changing roles and responsibilities. Specialists who previously relied on their own creativity and intuition may experience hesitation in delegating competencies to AI systems, perceiving it as a threat to their position or creative autonomy. The lack of a defined AI responsibility culture within an organization poses an additional obstacle; without clear, internal codes of conduct that specify the ethical boundaries of AI use in SMM, operational teams may unwittingly introduce systems that generate bias or violate social norms. Successful strategic implementation therefore requires not only the acquisition of new technical skills but, above all, a comprehensive redefinition of values and attitudes within the company (Borsci et al., 2023).

The link between algorithmic bias and communication ethics creates a barrier in the form of a threat to brand equity. Unethical or biased content, even if generated inadvertently by an algorithm, is ultimately attributed to the brand that published it. This can result not only in an immediate image crisis on social media but also in long-term reputational damage and loss of intangible assets. This risk is amplified by the scale and speed of AI—an ethical error is no longer an incident but can be multiplied and rapidly disseminated before human intervention is possible. Consequently, digital governance must prioritize safety checks and human-in-the-loop mechanisms to ensure that automation does not come at the expense of fundamental values and communication equality (Prahl & Goh, 2021).

Another significant obstacle is the barrier of adapting to dynamic societal expectations. Unlike stable technological regulations, social norms and ethical sensitivities evolve extremely rapidly on social media. AI systems, especially those trained on historical data, can struggle to keep up with these changes, leading to the generation of content that was neutral yesterday but is now perceived as inappropriate or offensive. This creates the barrier of constantly retraining models ethically and constantly calibrating their toxicity indicators to reflect current audience sensitivities. This requires organizations to establish a flexible yet rigorous AI Ethics Committee that constantly monitors cultural trends and adapts internal policies, thereby preventing a clash between technological performance and CSR requirements (Koplin, 2023).

While crucial to brand integrity, the discourse on ethical and cultural barriers must be complemented by an analysis of significant formal issues—namely, legal and regulatory barriers. The introduction of AI to SMM confronts gaps in the existing legal system and a complex array of international regulations.

A major legal issue is the unsettled legal status of AIGC. This applies particularly to IP and copyright issues. In many jurisdictions, it remains unclear whether a machine-generated product can be protected by copyright, and if so, who is the formal right holder—the creator of the prompt, the entity providing the AI model, or perhaps the organization that implemented the system. This uncertainty creates a real risk of IP infringement, especially in the context of using algorithm training data, which often contains copyrighted material. The lack of a clear legal framework prevents companies from conducting long-term and secure strategic planning of digital campaigns based on AIGC.

AI-generated disinformation and harmful content is a growing challenge. In the case of deepfakes, or so-called algorithmic hallucinations that lead to defamation or the spread of false information, legal systems struggle to determine who is responsible. The allocation of civil liability between the social media platform hosting the content and the brand that published it using an AI tool remains unclear. The need to implement indemnification mechanisms in contracts with AI providers is therefore becoming a critical operational requirement to minimize the financial and reputational risks associated with these unpredictable algorithmic outcomes (Medhat et al., 2025).

In a global context, the complexity of global compliance is a key barrier. Differences in approaches to AI and data protection between key markets—for example, the strict privacy approach resulting from the EU's GDPR versus other, more permissive regulatory models—create a patchwork of requirements that international social media strategies must meet. The need to constantly audit personal data collection and processing for targeting and personalization purposes, while simultaneously complying with local content regulations (e.g., advertising bans), poses a significant administrative and strategic burden. The lack of international legal harmonization is therefore a barrier to the smooth and scalable implementation of uniform, ethical, and strategic digital governance.

In the research conducted by the authors, a key element was identifying implementation barriers. The barrier analysis was divided into two segments: strategic and ethical. In the context of implementing strategic digital management (Question 13), respondents indicated the dominance of human and cultural factors: 65% of respondents cited a lack of specialized skills and knowledge as the greatest obstacle, highlighting the challenges associated with human capital in the digital era. Organizational indolence is equally important—55% indicated resistance to change and organizational inertia as a significant brake on innovation. Financial barriers, such as a lack of sufficient budget for tools and technologies, ranked only third, cited by 40%. This indicates that in mature organizations, culture and competencies, not cost alone, constitute the main problem. Similarly, in the area of implementing ethical digital management and digital responsibility, 60% of respondents considered the difficulty in precisely defining and enforcing ethical boundaries regarding the use of data and AI to be the greatest barrier. This result reflects the lack of clear industry standards and the rapid pace of technological development that outpaces regulations. Furthermore, 50% of companies report a lack of structured, internal digital ethics codes, forcing managers to improvise when making complex decisions. Finally, 30% of respondents emphasize that technological change outpaces regulatory frameworks, producing ongoing legal and ethical uncertainty.

An analysis of the barriers to implementing strategic and ethical digital management would be incomplete without a detailed discussion of technical, infrastructural, competency-based, and strategic obstacles. These constitute the physical and organizational framework within which both ethics and law must operate. First and foremost, integrating AI into SMM encounters significant technological and infrastructural barriers. Effective use of generative models and analytical systems requires high implementation and maintenance costs. Companies must invest not only in expensive licenses for advanced AI tools but also in the substantial computing power [often based on cloud infrastructure and graphics processing units (GPUs)] required to train, scale, and run these models. At the same time, challenges arise with technological integration: new AI solutions must be seamlessly integrated with existing, often heterogeneous, CRM systems, content scheduling platforms (SMM tools), and internal data warehouses.

Adding to these technical challenges is the critical issue of data quality and management. AI algorithms are dependent on the "garbage in, garbage out" principle: if training data are incomplete, low-quality, or, worse yet, biased, the system's output will be erroneous, inefficient, or biased. Achieving adequate scalability also becomes a challenge, as AI solutions that prove successful in the pilot phase often require a fundamental overhaul to support a real-time mass communication environment (Rocco, 2022).

Furthermore, the success of AI adoption is largely determined by competency and strategic barriers. Even the most advanced AI tools will prove useless without properly prepared teams. A key problem is the widening competency gap. Social media specialists are now required not only to possess marketing knowledge but also proficiency in prompt engineering (the ability to create precise instructions for AI) and AI governance (the ability to manage risk and oversee the ethical operation of systems). This shift in role, from contractor to AI curator and strategist, requires significant investment in training that will enable employees to critically evaluate algorithmic outputs and detect potential "hallucinations" or errors (Guriță, 2025).

The ultimate obstacle is often the lack of a coherent AI implementation strategy. Instead of pursuing an integrated, long-term vision for digital transformation, organizations sporadically purchase isolated tools that don't communicate with each other and don't contribute to core business goals. The lack of established strategic oversight, for example, in the form of an AI Ethical Audit Committee, results in a lack of mechanisms for regularly assessing the impact of algorithms on a brand's image and audience. Consequently, effective strategic digital management requires not only technological modernization but, above all, leaders capable of creating a new organizational culture that balances innovation with accountability.

Examples and case studies from different geographic and cultural regions

The development and implementation of AI in SMM are inextricably linked to differences in regulatory and ethical approaches across key global regions, generating fundamental contrasts in AI's strategic implementation. Analyzing this contrast, spanning Europe, the United States, and East Asia, is essential to understanding the global diversity of digital governance. The direction set by the EU focuses on regulatory rigor, rights-oriented ethics, and transparency. Examples include not only the GDPR, which restricts the use of personal data in targeting and training AI models, but also, and more importantly, the EU AI Act. This act introduces risk classifications for AI systems, which has direct implications for SMM tools; high-risk systems (e.g., those affecting access to services or engaging in discriminatory targeting) are subject to much stricter compliance requirements. From an SMM perspective, the European strategy forces brands to use AI explainability mechanisms (XAI) to justify why a given algorithm made a specific decision regarding content personalization or moderation, prioritizing ethics and consumer protection over pure market innovation.

A completely different approach characterizes the United States, where market liberalism and accelerated innovation prevail, with limited federal regulatory oversight. In the United States, the main driving force behind AI development is the private sector, and ethical and legal challenges are often addressed through civil lawsuits (especially regarding IP infringement and privacy claims in individual states) rather than through comprehensive, centralized legislation. In SMM, this favors the aggressive implementation of new technologies, such as advanced generative models and deepfakes in marketing campaigns, with less fear of immediate regulatory intervention. This means that brands operating in this market can achieve faster and more experimental AI implementations, but face higher risks of litigation and reputational damage in the event of ethical violations.

A third, highly differentiated model is presented by East Asian countries, with particular emphasis on China, where the priority is the integration of innovation with state oversight. In the context of SMM, AI systems are widely used for mass and deep personalization and behavioral data analysis (e.g., in apps like WeChat or Douyin), often without the stringent requirements for individual consent found in Europe. At the same time, AI implementation is subject to strict state control and content censorship requirements. In digital governance, this means that the main barrier is not a lack of trust in technology but the need to adapt algorithms to political and ideological requirements, which is crucial for companies wishing to maintain their presence in these markets (Yang & Yao, 2022).

As a result, these discrepancies force multinational corporations to avoid a single SMM strategy. Instead, they must operate within a framework of regulatory segmentation, where a strategy for EU markets must prioritize compliance and transparency (reducing regulatory risk), while a strategy for US markets might prioritize aggressive innovation (accepting higher legal and reputational risk), and for Asian markets, compliance with government oversight requirements. This diversity imposes high adaptation costs and poses a strategic barrier to global effectiveness.

The regulatory and ethical contrast between regions, while crucial, must be complemented by a detailed analysis of cultural differences in the acceptance of AIGC. The ability to effectively manage social media depends largely on how target audiences in different regions of the world respond to machine-generated messages. The first and fundamental barrier is the linguistic and localization challenge. While generative AI models have achieved high proficiency in languages with simple inflections, such as English, they encounter significant difficulties in handling languages with rich grammatical structures and complex cultural nuances, such as Polish, Hungarian, or Finnish. Automated content localization often leads to stylistic errors and a misunderstanding of the local memetic, humorous, or religious context, which ultimately results in image crises and a sense of disrespect for the recipient. In these cases, relying on AIGC as the primary source of communication generates greater risks than benefits, necessitating intensive human oversight of translation and cultural adaptation (Roche et al., 2023).

The language issue directly impacts the acceptance of authenticity in machine-generated content. There is a significant contrast between regions where consumers are culturally accustomed to highly formatted, synthetic AI communication and regions where authenticity is key and a distinctly human voice is required. For example, in some Asian markets, in which communication culture is often more formal and indirect, precise and esthetically refined AI-generated content is more likely to be accepted. However, in Western cultures, where spontaneity, originality, and emotional engagement are emphasized, brands must intentionally incorporate non-automated elements—e.g., unique behind-the-scenes stories or interactions led directly by key opinion leaders—to maintain loyalty and counteract the perception of impersonality.

Ultimately, these cultural dynamics create a barrier in the form of differences in sensitivity to ethical and social norms. What is acceptable or neutral in one region may be deeply offensive in another. AI systems, even those with built-in toxicity indicators, are trained on global datasets that may not reflect local, subtle cultural taboos. As a result, digital governance must be equipped with AI cultural adaptation mechanisms that constantly monitor and calibrate models for local sensitivity. The success of global SMM in the AI era, therefore, depends not only on technological efficiency but, crucially, on the capacity for cultural intelligence of algorithms and conscious, human oversight of what and how machines communicate (Sharma, 2025).

To determine the importance of an international perspective, the authors' research (described in Chapter 2) explored the importance of learning from examples and case studies from diverse geographic and cultural regions. The vast majority—80% of respondents—agreed or strongly agreed that this was crucial for effective strategy adaptation and building resilience. This finding provides a strong rationale for incorporating global and diverse examples into decision-making processes and supports the book's thesis on the importance of a holistic cultural approach to digital governance.

The conclusions drawn from the authors' research are as follows:

- Digital transformation is inevitable, and AI is a key element. The fact that as many as 80% of respondents are aware of or already using AI in SMM indicates the rapid pace of change. At the same time, the persistent 20% adoption gap, driven by knowledge and cost barriers, threatens to deepen the digital divide between market leaders and the rest of the world. Ultimately, organizational resilience in the future will be measured by the ability to ethically and strategically implement AI into key processes.
- It's important to emphasize that implementation barriers are primarily cultural and competency-based. The results clearly indicate that the greatest impediments to strategic and ethical change in the digital environment are not financial factors but rather soft factors: lack of specialized skills and knowledge (65%) and organizational resistance (55%). This suggests that digital transformation is primarily a cultural transformation, requiring leaders to systematically invest in training and actively manage change at all levels of the organization.
- Finally, a global perspective is seen as a strategic necessity. The dominant response (80%) in favor of learning from case studies from different geographic and cultural regions confirms that executives are seeking international ethical and strategic role models. This openness is essential to help companies navigate the dynamic and globally connected social media environment. Consequently, achieving sustainable resilience at the national level becomes impossible without strategic openness to global experiences and the adoption of best practices.

Continuing the analysis of barriers to implementing AI in SMM, it is necessary to delve deeper into the issue of economic and competency barriers, which in the European environment take on a specific and complex form, often constituting a greater obstacle than the cost of the technology itself. The key obstacle on the European continent is the cost and infrastructure barrier, although its nature is more nuanced than in developing countries. In Europe, especially in smaller Member States and the small and medium enterprises (SME) sector, the high investment costs of advanced AI tools and maintaining complex cloud infrastructure constitute a significant brake on innovation. While large corporations can afford the expensive licenses and computing power necessary to train and maintain large generative models, smaller entities often struggle with budget constraints. Moreover, the stringent requirements of the GDPR and the upcoming obligations arising from the EU AI Act increase compliance costs, forcing companies to invest not only in technology but also in specialized legal audits and transparency mechanisms, which constitutes an additional financial burden (European Commission, 2023).

The competency- and strategy-related barrier is becoming a key challenge in Europe. Despite generally high levels of education, many European countries face a significant gap in specialized AI governance and prompt engineering skills. Unlike the United States, where staff are dynamically trained in managing Big Data and AI models, European social media teams demonstrate cultural resistance to delegating creativity to machines. This shifts responsibility from performing tasks to overseeing and auditing AI systems, requiring companies to massively invest in staff retraining. The lack of these specific, advanced skills creates a substantial risk of suboptimal utilization of procured tools or, worse yet, heightened ethical risks arising from miscalibrated algorithms.

To fully understand the European context, it is necessary to contrast it with the challenges of the Global South. In developing countries, economic barriers take a more fundamental form: problems with access to reliable Internet infrastructure, power supply instability, and a lack of basic budgets for licenses and equipment dominate. These barriers are physical obstacles that prevent AI from scaling. Furthermore, many developing countries lack access to high-quality, sustainable training datasets in local languages and contexts, leading to algorithms biased toward the Global North. While Europe struggles for ethical and competent AI implementation, countries in the Global South are primarily grappling with barriers to access and basic technological infrastructure. This divergence means that a global AI governance strategy must address this dual battlefront: in Europe, regulatory and competency challenges predominate, while in the South, infrastructural and economic challenges predominate (UNESCO, 2021).

Analyzing barriers to AI implementation requires illustrating their practical consequences, which manifest themselves in ethical, legal, and competency spheres, threatening the coherence of a digital strategy. A practical manifestation of ethical barriers is the problem of replicating algorithmic bias in management processes. A classic example is the situation in which Amazon's recruitment algorithm had to be withdrawn because the system, learning from historical data, automatically discriminated against candidates (Dastin, 2018). This was a paradigmatic case of the "garbage in, garbage out" principle—the historical bias of training data was scaled up and automated, immediately violating the declared principles of equality. Simultaneously, this problem manifests itself in visual content: generative AI imagery tools consistently exhibit gender and racial bias when generating professional images, a critical barrier for brands aspiring to promote diversity on social media. Using such content without human-in-the-loop (human oversight) directly weakens brand equity (Bolukbasi et al., 2016).

Legal and regulatory barriers are reflected in the growing number of incidents related to disinformation and the unregulated status of the AIGC. A global challenge is posed by deepfake videos, in which high-profile figures, such as politicians, are used to promote fraudulent investment products. This type of automated manipulation creates immediate reputational risk and forces legal systems to determine who bears civil liability for damages—the creator, the platform, or the AI tool. This highlights the legal loophole regarding the AIGC's status. Furthermore, in high-stakes communications (e.g., official

statements), AI translation errors (so-called hallucinations) can lead to misinterpretation, which in local contexts (e.g., situations in India with condolence notes) is immediately attributed to the institution, causing a loss of trust and the immediate need to disable automated tools.

At the operational and strategic levels, competency barriers manifest themselves in internal cultural resistance and a lack of strategic vision. In many creative companies, marketing agencies and SMM departments report strong resistance to fully implementing AIGC tools, fearing loss of control over tone of voice and a degradation of their creative role. This lack of trust and knowledge is a key barrier, confirming that the problem is not a lack of tools but a lack of role transformation strategies. Organizations underinvest in AI governance and prompt engineering training, leading employees to perceive AI as a rival rather than a support. Without the creation of a skilled AI curator role, effective and ethical implementation of systems is impossible (He & Fang, 2024).

References

Bolukbasi, T., Chang, K. W., Zou, J. Y., Saligrama, V., & Kalai, A. T. (2016). Man is to computer programmer as woman is to homemaker? debiasing word embeddings. *Advances in Neural Information Processing Systems, 29.*

Borsci, S., Lehtola, V. V., Nex, F., Yang, M. Y., Augustijn, E. W., Bagheriye, L., Brune, C., Kounadi, O., Li, J., Moreira, J., van der Nagel, J., Veldkamp, B., Le, D. V., Wang, M., Wijnhoven, F., Wolterink, J., & Zurita-Milla, R. (2023). Embedding artificial intelligence in society: Looking beyond the EU AI master plan using the culture cycle. *AI & Society*, *38*(4), 1465–1484.

Dastin, J. (2018, October 11). Amazon scraps secret AI recruiting tool that showed bias against women. *Reuters*. https://www.reuters.com/article/world/insight-amazon-scraps-secret-ai-recruiting-tool-that-showed-bias-against-women-idUSKCN1MK0AG/ on line 23 November 2025

European Commission. (2023). *Artificial intelligence in the EU: Barriers, opportunities and adoption among SMEs*. Directorate-General for Communications Networks, Content and Technology.

Falgoust, G., Winterlind, E., Moon, P., Parker, A., Zinzow, H., & Madathil, K. C. (2022). Applying the uses and gratifications theory to identify motivational factors behind young adult's participation in viral social media challenges on TikTok. *Human Factors in Healthcare*, *2*, 100014.

Guriță, A. E. (2025, June). SAID: A social media AI-generated interface dataset using prompt engineering methods focused on accessibility. In *Proceedings of the international AAAI conference on web and social media* (Vol. 19, pp. 2446–2453).

He, X., & Fang, L. (2024). Regulatory challenges in synthetic media governance: Policy frameworks for AI-generated content across image, video, and social platforms. *Journal of Robotic Process Automation, AI Integration, and Workflow Optimization*, *9*(12), 36–54.

Koplin, J. J. (2023). Dual-use implications of AI text generation. *Ethics and Information Technology*, *25*(2), 32.

Lai, V., Carton, S., Bhatnagar, R., Liao, Q. V., Zhang, Y., & Tan, C. (2022). Human-ai collaboration via conditional delegation: A case study of content moderation. In *Proceedings of the 2022 CHI conference on human factors in computing systems* (pp. 1–18).

Medhat, M., Ayoub, L. W., Daher, M., & Mohamed, K. M. (2025). Ethical considerations in AI-generated content on social media. In *Sustainable data management: Navigating big data, communication technology, and business digital leadership* (Vol. 1, pp. 611–620). Springer Nature Switzerland.

Napoli, P. M., & Adi, S. (2025). On moving fast and breaking things . . . again: Social media's lessons for generative AI governance. *Information, Communication & Society*, 1–17.

Prahl, A., & Goh, W. W. P. (2021). "Rogue machines" and crisis communication: When AI fails, how do companies publicly respond?. *Public Relations Review*, *47*(4), 102077.

Ramkumar, N. (2025). AI-powered social media content optimization: Enhancing engagement, personalization, and efficiency. In *2025 International conference on computing technologies & data communication (ICCTDC)* (pp. 1–10). IEEE.

Rocco, G. (2022). Garbage in, garbage out. *European Journal of Cardio-Thoracic Surgery*, *61*(5), 1020–1021.

Roche, C., Wall, P. J., & Lewis, D. (2023). Ethics and diversity in artificial intelligence policies, strategies and initiatives. *AI and Ethics*, *3*(4), 1095–1115.

Sahebi, S., & Formosa, P. (2025). The AI-mediated communication dilemma: Epistemic trust, social media, and the challenge of generative artificial intelligence. *Synthese*, *205*(3), 1–24.

Sharma, N. (2025). Role of artificial intelligence in intercultural dialogue and language: Ethical frame works for sustainability and equity. In *Innovative multidisciplinary approaches to global challenges: Sustainability, equity, and ethics in an interconnected world* (IMASEE 2025) (pp. 215–223). Atlantis Press.

UNESCO. (2021). *AI and low-resource languages: Addressing the needs of the global south.* United Nations Educational, Scientific and Cultural Organization.

Yang, F., & Yao, Y. (2022). A new regulatory framework for algorithm-powered recommendation services in China. *Nature Machine Intelligence*, *4*(10), 802–803.

Index

For Product Safety Concerns and Information please contact our EU representative GPSR@taylorandfrancis.com Taylor & Francis Verlag GmbH, Kaufingerstraße 24, 80331 München, Germany